SCHOLASTIC

WITHDRAWN

20 JUN 2023

Terms and conditions

IMPORTANT – PERMITTED USE AND WARNINGS – READ CAREFULLY BEFORE USING

IF YOU ACCEPT THE ABOVE CONDITIONS YOU MAY PROCEED TO USE THE CD-ROM.

Recommended system requirements:

- Windows: XP (Service Pack 3), Vista (Service Pack 2) or Windows 7 with 2.33GHz processor
- Mac: OS 10.6 to 10.8 with Intel Core™ Duo processor
- 1GB RAM (recommended)
- 1024 x 768 Screen resolution
- CD-ROM drive (24x speed recommended)
- 16-bit sound card
- Microsoft Word

For all technical support queries, please phone   0845 6039091.

SCHOLASTIC

Book End, Range Road, Witney, Oxfordshire, OX29 0YD
www.scholastic.co.uk
© 2014, Scholastic Ltd

23456789 4567890123

British Library Cataloguing-in-Publication Data
A catalogue record for this book is available from the
British Library.

ISBN 978-1407-12861-0
Printed by Bell & Bain Ltd, Glasgow

Authors
Zoe Ross and Steve Bunce

Editorial team
Mark Walker, Jenny Wilcox and Angela Aylmore

Cover Design
Andrea Lewis

Design Team
Shelley Best and Andrea Lewis

Contents

Introduction

Computing is a subject full of opportunities for children to develop their thinking, with practical programming skills, focused on real world examples. The new 'Computing' curriculum replaces the old 'ICT' curriculum, which was disapplied in September 2012. This planning guide is designed to help support schools, subject coordinators and teachers to navigate the new National Curriculum and to plan for their own school curriculum.

> 'The National Curriculum for Computing aims to ensure that all pupils:
> - can understand and apply the fundamental principles and concepts of computer science, including abstraction, logic, algorithms and data representation
> - can analyse problems in computational terms, and have repeated practical experience of writing computer programs in order to solve such problems
> - can evaluate and apply information technology, including new or unfamiliar technologies, analytically to solve problems
> - are responsible, competent, confident and creative users of information and communication technology.'
> (DfE, 2013)

The National Curriculum Programme of Study for Computing contains guidance for Key Stages 1 and 2, and therefore careful thought needs to be given to progression through each year group. The *100 Computing Lessons* series offers one title for Years 1 and 2, one for Years 3 and 4 and one for Years 5 and 6. Within each book, you will find planning for each year group, divided into six blocks, to correspond with the half term periods. The books can be used flexibly to suit your teaching and the children's learning, for example, moving the topics into a different order in a year or using materials from the years above and below. The content introduces computing concepts with many practical examples, so it is important to match it to your pupils' abilities.

The subject focuses on computational thinking with an emphasis on programming. In addition, there are other areas of computing which have equal importance. In this series, the National Curriculum has been divided into four key subject areas:

- Algorithms and programming
- Data and information
- How computers work
- Communication and e-safety

The 'Algorithms and programming' parts of the programme of study have been combined into one block, as they are closely related and there is a progression over the key stages. Each year there are two 'Algorithms and programming' blocks and one each for 'Data and information', 'How computers work', 'Communication' and 'E-safety'.

Terminology

In this guide, the main terms used are:

- **Subject areas:** the area of the subject, for computing, we will use 'Algorithms and programming', 'Data and information', 'How computers work' and 'Communication and e-safety'.
- **Objectives:** by the end of Key Stage 1 and Key Stage 2, children are expected to know, apply and understand the matters, skills and processes detailed in the relevant programme of study.

The new computing curriculum has terminology that may be new to many teachers, for example, 'abstraction'. It is important to introduce the new words and concepts and reinforce the learning. The 'Background knowledge' sections will support the learning of these terms, as the series progresses.

Assessment

During each half term, the lessons can be delivered one per week and assessment opportunities are integrated into them. At the end of each of the blocks there is an assessment lesson that reinforces the learning and provides more open-ended tasks for the children to attempt. Guidance is given to support the observation and questioning of the children.

About the book

The book provides content for each year group (Years 1–6) and includes:

- **Long-term planning:** An overview of the subject areas and which objectives should be covered in that year. These are based upon the statutory guidance from the curriculum – written in black text (DfE, 2013). They are supported by non-statutory guidance from the British Computer Society – written in grey text (BCS, 2013).
- **Overview of progression:** This is a year-by-year overview of how the children progress through the subject areas. The progression overview includes what children should already know from the previous year, what's covered in the current year and how this progresses into the following year.
- **Medium-term planning:** Six half-termly grids are provided for each year group. Each contains an overview of each week's planning including the theme being covered, the outcomes for that week and the objectives covered.
- **Background knowledge:** This explains key concepts, relevant to the year group, to help support teachers' knowledge of computing.

Equipment

Many of the lesson activities can be carried out away from the computer, for example, through classroom games or paper-based tasks. When using computers, schools may have a range of devices, for example, desktops, laptops, cloud-computing laptops, netbooks and tablets. In *100 Computing Lessons*, free software and websites are used, in addition to the interactive resources.

About the CD-ROM

The CD-ROM provides the Long-term planning, Overview of progression, Medium-term planning and Background knowledge as editable word files. These can be used and adapted to meet the needs of your school. There is a simple menu screen on the CD-ROM, simply navigate to the year group you require and then click on the button to open the associated file.

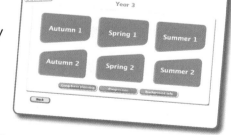

About the poster

The poster summarises the progression of key concepts in the Computing National Curriculum. Display it in a central location, such as the staffroom, to help improve understanding of the new curriculum within your school.

Year 1 Long-term planning

ALGORITHMS AND PROGRAMMING

The National Curriculum states that children should be taught to:

- understand what algorithms are; how they are implemented as programs on digital devices; and that programs execute by following precise and unambiguous instructions

---

- Children should be taught that an algorithm is a precise way of solving a problem.
- Children will be familiar with following instructions from their teachers and rules when playing games. They should extend this knowledge to recognise and give examples of algorithms in everyday life.
- Through testing different algorithms, children should learn to create their own algorithms for specific purposes. They should then refine the steps to ensure that they are clear and easy to follow.
- Children should be shown that algorithms can be followed by humans and also by computers and they need precise, unambiguous instructions.

HOW COMPUTERS WORK

The National Curriculum states that children should be taught to:

- recognise common uses of information technology beyond school

---

- Most children will have experienced using computers in the Reception year, nursery or at home. There are different types of computers, such as desktop, laptop and tablet and they will be able to recognise these.
- Through exploration in school, the children will be able to name places where desktop and laptop computers are used. They need to learn that other devices contain computers, for example, the photocopier or DVD player.
- Outside of school, the children should develop an understanding of common uses of computers, for example, mobile phones, supermarket checkout tills and in other places they visit.
- Children need to be able to name the parts of a computer and describe its simple functions.

DATA AND INFORMATION

The National Curriculum states that children should be taught to:

- use technology purposefully to organise digital content

- In everyday life, children will have experienced digital content through photographs, videos and music. This content can be organised in different ways. In order to do this, the children need to be able to recognise different types of content and name them.
- Through practice, children should learn that digital content can be manipulated by grouping different types together, for example, text and images or audio and images.
- Children need to be taught how to organise and manipulate the digital content purposefully.

COMMUNICATION AND E-SAFETY

The National Curriculum states that children should be taught to:

- use technology safely and respectfully, keeping personal information private; identify where to go for help and support when they have concerns about content or contact on the internet or other online technologies

---

- Children will be familiar with sharing information about themselves, such as, name, age, address and interests. They need to be taught that sometimes they need to keep information private. They need to be shown through careful examples when it is appropriate to share and with whom.
- In school, the children have friends they talk to and play games with. They are aware of the concept of friends and how they should behave towards each other. However, this is not always borne out in practice. Therefore, they should identify the characteristics of a 'good' friend and how they behave. This learning is then transferred to communicating with friends online and how they should behave towards one another.
- Children should be taught who to ask for help and support, whether at home or at school, if they have concerns or are worried by something they see on a computer.

Overview of progression in Year 1

Algorithms and programming

In Year 1, children will begin with very simple lists of instructions, delivered through familiar contexts, such as, 'Simon says' games. The children will develop their use of instructions to show how they can be combined to perform more complex tasks, laying the foundations for programming in Year 2.

With algorithms, it is important that the children start to develop sequences of instructions that are accurate – for example, when putting on shoes it is important to stress that there are two instructions, for the left and right foot, rather than just saying 'put on shoes'. This will prepare the children for creating detailed sequences of instructions and 'debugging' algorithms, and programs in the following years, and is an important skill to develop.

When the children are focusing on their instructions, try to make links to their learning about sentences in English. For example, a sentence must contain at least one verb and a subject; a capital letter is found at the start of the sentence and a full stop at the end. There is a strong need in both English and computing for precision in creating clear instructions.

Linking to the mathematics curriculum, the children will be learning about sequencing numbers. For example, a list of instructions can be numbered and then 'jumbled up'; the task is then to order them numerically. An understanding of place value is important in this example and can be supported using number lines and 100 squares.

Data and information

The children's vocabularies will be extended through discussion and by focusing on new words from their reading and listening. They begin with identifying data types within a dinosaur theme, such as name and size. They move on to recognising types of data, for example, text, image, video and sound. This is important for subsequent years, where they will be identifying file types, for example, txt, jpg, wmv and mp3. This learning is reinforced through the English curriculum, for example, by identifying pronouns and letter patterns.

Children progress in mathematics by recognizing simple patterns in data and then processing the information to represent it in different ways. For example, they can order the dinosaurs from smallest to largest and vice versa. They move on to recognise the digits in the data and name them; this prepares them for naming large numbers in the hundreds and thousands ranges.

How computers work

During Year 1, children will begin to name the parts of a computer and what they do, using nouns and adjectives. They also create models of a computer, offering opportunities for speaking and listening as they role-play using each part and explain what it does.

Children then begin to recognise that computers can be found in different devices both inside and outside of school, from desktop computers to DVD players, mobile phones and checkout tills.

Communication and e-safety

In Year 1, the children focus on communicating information from a story. They read the story and retell it to each other and begin to consider how they can share the story digitally. They use a variety of techniques to capture their stories including the use of photos, video and audio; this links very clearly with the English curriculum and will in particular help to develop speaking and listening skills.

Progression in e-safety begins with identifying 'What is personal information?'. Reflecting upon the 'Data' and 'Information' lessons, they will know about names and facts about dinosaurs, so they can identify similar pieces of data about themselves. This enables the children to use pronouns, verbs and adjectives to create sentences about themselves. These effective comprehension techniques will then be built upon in Year 2 and subsequent years.

To develop an understanding about e-safety, the children consider with whom they should share information, in-person or online. They should know who to tell if they have concerns and this should link to the school's own policies and procedures for e-safety.

Medium-term planning Autumn 1: Dinosaurs

National Curriculum objective

Children should be taught to:
- use technology purposefully to create, organise and manipulate digital content

W	Outcomes	Objectives
1	Can identify the names of dinosaurs. Can describe the different characteristics of dinosaurs.	• To identify the name of the dinosaur. • To identify the size of the dinosaur. • To identify the characteristics of a dinosaur, for example, scales, tail, teeth.
2	Can sort the dinosaurs in simple ways. Can categorise the dinosaurs into groups.	• To sort the names alphabetically. • To sort the dinosaurs in order of size, from largest to smallest and from smallest to largest. • To group by characteristics, for example, horns, wings.
3	Can describe and use basic types of data. Can combine images and audio data types in simple ways.	• To identify the basic data types of image, video, audio and text. • To match images and audio data types using a simple drag and drop activity.
4	Can combine text and image data for a particular purpose.	• To draw their favourite dinosaur, add a text name and simple text description.
5	Can collect and organise data.	• To collect data using a tally sheet.
6	Can manipulate data in graphical formats.	• To display data using simple pictograms.
Assess and review		• To assess the half-term's work.

Medium-term planning Autumn 2: Traditional stories

National Curriculum objective

Children should be taught to:
• understand what algorithms are

W	Outcomes	Objectives
1	Can follow a sequence of instructions. Can verbally give instructions for someone else to follow.	• To be able to follow a series of simple instructions through games. • To participate in giving instructions for others to follow. • To know that instructions can be given in a number of different ways (for example, verbally and using images and text).
2	Can understand that instructions need to be accurate. Can rearrange a sequence of instructions.	• To identify incorrectly sequenced instructions. • To predict what will happen if incorrectly sequenced instructions are followed. • To sequence instructions into the correct order.
3	Can discuss why stories need to be in the correct order. Can reorganise stories and number sequences into the correct order.	• To identify the beginning, middle and end of traditional stories. • To identify errors in the sequencing of traditional stories. • To sequence traditional stories into the correct order.
4	Can solve simple logic problems. Can verbally describe solutions to problems.	• To begin to know strategies to solve simple logic problems. • To be able to solve simple logic problems successfully (independently or in pairs). • To explain in simple terms the steps taken to solve simple logic problems.
5	Can plan a series of instructions. Can check the accuracy of a series of instructions.	• To be able to create a simple image plan of a sequence of instructions. • To compare the plan created by the children with a prepared plan and make adjustments, as necessary. • To follow pictorial plans to complete simple tasks.
6	Can explain that an algorithm is a precise way of solving a problem. Can explain that algorithms need to be accurate, so a computer can execute them.	• To learn that an 'algorithm' is a term used to describe a sequence of instructions for a computer to follow. • To create algorithms for human robots. • To understand why algorithms should be accurate. • To predict what might happen if given algorithms are inaccurate.
Assess and review		• To assess the half-term's work.

Medium-term planning Spring 1: Computers in everyday life

National Curriculum objective

Children should be taught to:
- recognise common uses of information technology beyond school

W	Outcomes	Objectives
1	Can name parts of the classroom computer. Can describe how to use the keyboard, mouse and screen.	• To learn the names of basic parts of the computer using simple songs and rhymes. • To be able to name mouse, screen, keyboard and CPU. • To explain, in simple terms, the functions of the main parts of a computer.
2	Can explain that a mouse is an input device. Can use a mouse to complete simple tasks.	• To learn that a mouse is an input device that controls a pointer on the screen. • To learn that a mouse allows a user to control elements on the screen. • To become more confident using a mouse when completing simple tasks.
3	Can explain that a keyboard is an input device. Can accurately use a keyboard to type simple sentences.	• To learn that a keyboard is an input device that allows a user to input letters, numbers and symbols. • To become more confident using a keyboard by typing simple words and sentences combining numbers, letters and symbols.
4	Can explain that a screen is an output device. Can recognise the common features of different types of computer screens.	• To learn that a screen is an output device that displays information for the user. • To be able to explain what they can usually expect to see on a screen.
5	Can understand in simple terms how a CPU works. Can explain that a CPU follows instructions.	• To learn that a CPU contains the computer 'brain'. • To be able to explain that a CPU processes instructions given by input devices. • To be able to explain that a CPU gives instructions to output devices.
6	Can build a simple computer model. Can explain in simple terms the main parts of a computer and how a computer works.	• To know the main parts of a computer. • To verbally explain the main parts of a computer. • To identify input and output devices on a simple computer model. • To identify the CPU and explain how it works in simple terms.
Assess and review		• To assess the half-term's work.

Medium-term planning Spring 2: Plants and animals

National Curriculum objective

Children should be taught to:
- understand what algorithms are, how they are implemented as programs on digital devices, and that programs execute by following precise and unambiguous instructions

W	Outcomes	Objectives
1	Can rearrange a sequence of images into the correct order. Can identify and correct errors within a sequence of images.	• To rearrange images into the correct sequence. • To explain verbally the reasons behind their choice of sequencing. • To identify and correct errors in sequencing. • To be introduced to the term 'debugging'.
2	Can create sequences of images in the correct order. Can explain why accuracy is important and how they debug their work.	• To create a sequence of images. • To identify and correct errors in sequences of images. • To know and understand the term 'debugging'. • To understand the importance of accurate sequences.
3	Can use simple flowcharts to represent instructions. Can identify and represent repetition in flowcharts.	• To know what a flowchart is and understand how it can be followed. • To rearrange a simple flowchart into the correct order. • To debug their own and others' flowcharts. • To identify and represent repetition in a flowchart.
4	Can explain that algorithms need to be accurate so they can be followed. Can create simple algorithms to control an object.	• To be able to explain that an algorithm is a term used to describe a sequence of instructions for a computer to follow. • To create simple, accurate algorithms to move an object. • To explain how they have created their algorithms to ensure accuracy. • To be able to debug algorithms to ensure accuracy.
5	Can control an onscreen device. Can give instructions and predict the outcome.	• To control an onscreen device. • To predict what will happen when controlling an onscreen device. • To give instructions accurately to an onscreen device. • To begin to understand that a computer program executes an algorithm.
6	Can control an onscreen device using precise instructions to achieve a specific goal. Can debug instructions to ensure a specific goal is achieved.	• To control an onscreen device accurately. • To predict what will happen when controlling an onscreen device. • To give instructions to an onscreen device to achieve specific goals. • To be able to spot errors and debug instructions to achieve specific goals. • To begin to understand that a computer program executes an algorithm.
Assess and review		• To assess the half-term's work.

Medium-term planning Summer 1: 'Handa's Surprise'

National Curriculum objective

Children should be taught to:
- use technology purposefully to create, organise and manipulate digital content

W	Outcomes	Objectives
1	Can sequence a series of events into the correct order.	• To identify the correct order of a story. • To be able to explain and describe the beginning, middle and end of a story. • To be able to sequence a story into the correct order. • To create a simple, pictorial storyboard, retelling a story in the correct order.
2	Can follow a sequence of instructions. Can use digital cameras to capture content.	• To role-play a sequence in a story. • To capture role-play, using a simple digital camera. • To work effectively in small groups.
3	Can use audio devices to record accompanying music.	• To role-play a sequence in a story. • To capture role-play, using a simple digital audio device (microphone). • To work effectively in small groups.
4	Can use audio devices to record narration.	• To role-play a sequence in a story. • To capture role-play, using a simple digital audio device (microphone). • To work effectively in small groups.
5	Can use digital cameras to capture video content.	• To role-play a sequence in a story. • To capture role-play, using a simple digital camera. • To work effectively in small groups.
6	Can combine digital content purposefully. Can understand that images, audio and video can be combined effectively.	• To learn that images, audio and video can be combined using software. • To evaluate images, audio and video and give simple feedback.
Assess and review		• To assess the half-term's work.

Medium-term planning Summer 2: Sea and coast

National Curriculum objective

Children should be taught to:
- keep personal information private
- identify where to go for help and support when they have concerns about content or contact on the internet or other online technologies

W	Outcomes	Objectives
1	Can identify what makes a good friend both off and online. Can identify features of appropriate behaviour online.	• To list what makes a 'good' friend. • To identify how 'good' friends communicate through role-play. • To discuss methods of face-to-face communication. • To discuss methods of communication that are not face-to-face (for example, letters, postcards, email, *Facebook*).
2	Can create a list using text. Can order a list alphabetically and numerically.	• To create a list (for example, objects you would see at the seaside). • To identify and discuss how to stay safe at different physical locations. • To begin to understand how to stay safe when online.
3	Can protect their identity online by not using their full name. Can protect their identity online by choosing an avatar.	• To understand how to behave positively with others when face-to-face and online. • To learn how to protect private information when online (for example, considering when to share address details).
4	Can create a secure password and understand the need to protect it.	• To create a memorable password that is not easily identified by others. • To understand why passwords need to be kept private.
5	Can create a list of websites that the children visit and sort, in order of popularity. Can understand the need for accuracy when entering website addresses.	• To create a list of websites. • To sort a list based on one criteria. • To stay safe by accurately entering the website address. • To understand what to do if they visit a website they don't recognise.
6	Can write a poem based on staying safe online.	• To begin to understand how to stay safe when online.
Assess and review		• To assess the half-term's work.

Year 1 Background knowledge

The new computing curriculum offers many opportunities for children to develop their thinking and their early knowledge of computers. They bring a wide and varied experience of problem solving to the classroom and it is important they share this with the other children.

Computational thinking

The National Curriculum for computing follows the fundamentals of computational thinking, which is a problem-solving process. Computational thinking can involve:

- formulating problems in a way that enables us to use computers to help solve them
- logically organising and analysing data
- representing data through abstractions, such as models and simulations
- automating solutions through algorithmic thinking (a series of ordered steps)
- identifying, analysing, and implementing possible solutions with the goal of achieving the most efficient and effective combination of steps and resources
- generalising and transferring problem-solving processes to a wide variety of problems.

Reference: ISTE (2013)

The *100 Computing Lessons* series follows the National Curriculum and highlights the use of computational thinking throughout the learning journey.

Algorithms and programming

An algorithm is a step-by-step list of instructions, which can be followed precisely, to solve a problem. Children use algorithms every day, for example, getting dressed, putting their clothes on in the correct order etc. Also, many games, such as, 'Simon Says', follow a set of instructions. In computational thinking, algorithms are sets of instructions to solve problems. They are then executed by computers using programs. In Key Stage 1, developing the core skills of creating and following instructions are the building blocks for later work.

Data and information

From an early stage, children are bombarded by data and information. Data can include names of people and objects, sounds, images and numbers. Children will have sorted data in nursery and in Reception, by using various characteristics. In Year 1 computing, they encounter dinosaurs and organise and manipulate the data, based on their prior experiences. It is important to address any misconceptions as they demonstrate their understanding of sorting and recognising the types of data. In computational thinking, this involves the logical organising of the data. In Year 2, they will develop their analytical skills using data.

How computers work

Children may have encountered computers at home, nursery or during their Reception Year. This could be through using desktops, laptops, tablets or accessing different games and activities on a smart phone. It is important for them to recognise the parts of the computer and begin to understand their functions. Most children will be able to name the mouse and keyboard of a desktop computer and may have different names for the screen, but still understand that it is for displaying the information. However, they might have difficulty in finding the CPU, memory and hard drive and saying what they do; this may be because those components are integrated into the screen or that they have never considered the 'big box' under the screen or on the floor. In Year 1, the children build a cardboard box representation of a desktop computer and learn the names and basic functions of the parts. They also begin to recognise computers in everyday life, such as mobile phones, washing machines and checkout shopping tills.

Communication and e-safety

The children are familiar with sharing information about themselves, such as, name, age, where they live. In Year 1, the children are asked to consider keeping some information private; this is in preparation for Year 2, when they consider the differences between sharing in-person and online. It also lays the foundations for looking for help and support when they find content which might worry or upset them.

SCHOLASTIC

Year 2 Long-term planning

ALGORITHMS AND PROGRAMMING

The National Curriculum states that children should be taught to:

- understand what algorithms are; how they are implemented as programs on digital devices; and that programs execute by following precise and unambiguous instructions
- create and debug simple programs
- use logical reasoning to predict the behaviour of simple programs

- In Year 2, children start to develop accuracy with their algorithms. They experiment and discover how to make the steps more clear, so that they can be followed precisely.
- Computers can also follow algorithms, as well as humans. Children should understand that any errors or ambiguity in their instructions could lead to the computer not giving the correct outputs.
- Children should be encouraged to persevere with problem solving and detecting errors (debugging the program).
- Drawing on their experiences of using algorithms, the children should try to predict the behaviour of simple programs, for example, function machines or floor robots.

HOW COMPUTERS WORK

The National Curriculum states that children should be taught to:

- recognise common uses of information technology beyond school

- Children might draw on their experiences of using computers, to describe the features and functions of their main parts. Their explanations should be a progression from Year 1, as they now have a more developed vocabulary and understanding of computers.
- Children should be taught about the more 'hidden' features of the main computer, for example, the CPU (Central Processing Unit), the memory and the hard drive.
- Making analogies can help the children conceptually understand difficult concepts, such as, where is the information stored? They should also be taught that the information can be stored in different formats, for example, a movie can be in wmv, mov or mp4 format.

DATA AND INFORMATION

The National Curriculum states that children should be taught to:

- use technology purposefully to create, organise, store, manipulate and retrieve digital content

- Building on the previous year, the children will use digital content in different ways. They will have organised and manipulated content, using simple examples. They should now be shown how to create digital content.
- Children will be able to collect data, using simple tally charts, and manipulate it into pictograms. This should be carried out using a real-world, relevant context.
- When teaching about storing digital content, the children may have experienced 'saving' and 'loading' a file in a computer program, such as *Paint* or a word processor. They need to consider where the digital content is kept and also if they are able to find that location at a later date.
- Outside of school, children may be familiar with saving progress in a video game. The teacher can bring that example into the lesson to help them understand the concepts of storing and retrieving digital content.

COMMUNICATION AND E-SAFETY

The National Curriculum states that children should be taught to:

- use technology safely and respectfully, keeping personal information private; identify where to go for help and support when they have concerns about content or contact on the internet or other online technologies

- In Year 2, the children are developing their understanding of the world around them and also the online world. They may not be using email or social media, but many children will be familiar with going online and searching the web. It is important therefore that they understand the benefits of going online and also how to stay safe.
- Using technology respectfully is important, as the children can see and read body language when face-to-face; they cannot when communicating by text online. They therefore need to know that the same rules apply to communicating online in a kind and friendly manner.
- Reinforcing the message from Year 1 and into Year 3, the children need to know who to go to for help and support, if they find content or have contact that makes them uncomfortable.

Overview of progression in Year 2

Algorithms and programming

In Year 2, the children build on their understanding that algorithms are a series of step-by-step instructions that solve a problem and make use of simple flowcharts for the first time. They are also introduced to controlling on-screen devices using simple sequences of instructions and create algorithms to achieve specific outcomes, for example repeating patterns or geometrical shapes. Logical thinking will be developed through activities, such as how to achieve the optimum planting pattern, using the 'Oliver's Vegetables' theme.

The main progression from Year 1 is the introduction of programming. The children have created algorithms for humans to follow and now they try them with computers by controlling simple on-screen devices and floor robots. By 'things going wrong' with the expected outputs of the programs, they learn that the computer follows instructions exactly, unlike humans. The children therefore begin to develop the accuracy of their instructions to ensure the correct outputs. In addition to creating precise programs, they will 'debug' the programs, identifying errors and correcting them. This is a skill used by adult programmers and so it is vital that the children learn this and consolidate the skill in subsequent year groups.

The 100 Computing Lessons link with English through retelling stories and sequencing events in the correct order. Children expand noun phrases to describe and specify the instructions. They also develop the skills and processes essential to writing, i.e. thinking aloud as they collect ideas, drafting and re-reading to check their meaning is clear.

In mathematics, the children will recognise the place value of each digit in a two-digit number, compare and order numbers from 0 to 100 and identify 2D shapes and patterns. In creating simple programs, they will solve problems in contexts. In addition, they use mathematical vocabulary to describe position, direction and movement.

Data and information

In Year 1, the children organised and manipulated data through a 'Dinosaur' theme. In Year 2, they use a 'Habitats' theme to collect, organise and manipulate the data. The lessons link to the mathematics curriculum by using branching databases to sort data and construct tally charts, block graphs and simple tables. They ask and answer simple questions, for example, finding the number of items in a category. Linking to English, the children understand books by asking and answering questions, using statements and describing non-fiction stories that are structured in different ways.

In addition to the use of data, the children begin to learn about storing and retrieving digital content, for example, saving a piece of work in the correct place and then retrieving it.

How computers work

During Year 2, the children will develop their knowledge of computers outside of school. They use a zoo theme, to explore the parts of a zoo and make analogies with the structure inside a computer's CPU. Linking to English, the children can write about real-life events, such as going to the zoo and using maps, then develop their non-fiction writing to describe the functions of the parts of the computer. Using positional language and the properties of shape in the descriptions will support the teaching in the mathematics curriculum.

Communication and e-safety

In Year 2, the communication and e-safety curriculum is delivered using a pirate theme to engage the children. They will consider their personal information and how they present themselves in person and when communicating through technology. In English this is developed through making inferences on what is being said and done and taking turns to share thoughts.

The lessons build on the learning from Year 1 about who they consider to be a friend and what pieces of information should be shared. Work in this area reinforces the message that, if they find content or have contact with someone that makes them concerned, then they know where to get help.

Medium-term planning Autumn 1: *Oliver's Vegetables*

National Curriculum objectives

Children should be taught to:
- understand what algorithms are; how they are implemented as programs on digital devices; and that programs execute by following precise and unambiguous instructions
- create and debug simple programs
- use logical reasoning to predict the behaviour of simple programs

W	Outcomes	Objectives
1	Can use simple flowcharts to represent instructions. Can identify and represent repetition in flowcharts.	• To know what a flowchart is and understand how it can be followed. • To arrange a simple flowchart into the correct order. • To use 'repeat', 'repeat until' and 'wait until' instructions within a flowchart. • To debug their own and others' flowcharts.
2	Can identify flowchart algorithms to create common shapes. Can debug flowchart algorithms.	• To be able to identify algorithms represented in flowcharts that will create 2D shapes. • To identify and correct errors in flowchart algorithms. • To understand how repetition can be used in flowcharts and algorithms to achieve a specific goal.
3	Can follow simple algorithms with accuracy. Can explain that algorithms need to be accurate and precise so they can be implemented.	• To follow simple algorithms to plant vegetables in specific patterns. • To begin to understand that computers need more accurate instructions than humans. • To begin to understand that computers use programs to implement algorithms.
4	Can control an onscreen device using a simple program. Can create programs to achieve specific goals.	• To control an onscreen device. • To predict what will happen when controlling an onscreen device. • To give instructions accurately to an onscreen device. • To begin to understand that a computer program executes an algorithm.
5	Can create simple algorithms to achieve specific goals. Can debug algorithms.	• To write simple algorithms to create specified patterns. • To control an onscreen device accurately in order to test their algorithms. • To be able to spot errors and debug algorithms and programs. • To begin to understand that a computer program executes an algorithm.
6	Can create simple, accurate and precise algorithms. Can test and debug algorithms.	• To create simple accurate algorithms using images and/or text. • To test and debug others' algorithms. • To understand that a computer program executes an algorithm.
Assess and review		• To assess the half-term's work.

Medium-term planning Autumn 2: Fairy Tales

National Curriculum objectives

Children should be taught to:
- understand what algorithms are; how they are implemented as programs on digital devices; and that programs execute by following precise and unambiguous instructions
- create and debug simple programs
- use logical reasoning to predict the behaviour of simple programs

W	Outcomes	Objectives
1	Can move a floor robot in simple ways. Can program a floor robot to reach a specified position.	• To understand that a programmable robot can be controlled by pressing buttons. • To predict what will happen when programming a floor robot. • To be able to give simple instructions to a programmable robot, including moving forwards, backwards, left and right turns. • To program a floor robot to reach specified positions.
2	Can program a floor robot with a sequence of instructions in order to achieve specific goals Can debug a simple program.	• To give simple sequences of instructions to a programmable floor robot. • To program a floor robot to follow the specific sequence of a story. • To identify and correct errors in programs (debugging).
3	Can program a floor robot with sequences of instructions. Can debug a program.	• To program a floor robot with devised sequences of instructions. • To test and debug a programmed algorithm to achieve an intended goal. • To be creative and experimental.
4	Can plan, implement, test and debug an algorithm to achieve a specific goal. Can begin to understand that a computer program within a floor robot executes an algorithm.	• To plan an algorithm to allow a floor robot to reach a specific goal in the most efficient way. • To program a floor robot with sequences of instructions to follow a planned path. • To test and rewrite their algorithm as necessary to achieve a specific goal (debugging). • To being to understand how the floor robot executes an algorithm.
5	Can use problem solving and logical thinking to program multiple floor robots, debugging them as necessary to follow a chosen path. Can explain how the wrote an algorithm and programmed a floor robot in simple terms.	• To use problem solving and logical thinking skills to plan the best algorithm for a robot to take to achieve a specific goal. • To plan an algorithm to allow a floor robot to reach a specific goal in the most efficient way. • To program two floor robots with sequences of instructions to follow a planned path. • To test and rewrite algorithms as necessary to achieve their goal (debugging). • To explain verbally how they chose the best algorithm and programmed their robot.
6	Can confidently program a floor robot to follow a path in the most efficient way. Can use problem solving and logical thinking to quickly and effectively debug their algorithm. Can begin to evaluate their own work.	• To be creative, experimental and work cooperatively with their peers. • To use problem solving and logical thinking skills to plan the best algorithm for a robot to take to follow a planned path in the most efficient way. • To explain verbally how they chose the best algorithm and programmed their robot. • To explain how they would change their approach in the future.
Assess and review		• To assess the half-term's work.

Medium-term planning Spring 1: Zoos

National Curriculum objective

Children should be taught to:
- recognise common uses of information technology beyond school

W	Outcomes	Objectives
1	Can name parts of the classroom computer. Can describe how the children use the keyboard, mouse and screen.	• To identify the main parts of a computer. • To name the main parts of a computer. • To describe the function of the main parts of a computer.
2	Can identify that a computer follows instructions. Can explain the basic function of the CPU and memory.	• To know that a computer follows instructions. • To explain the basic functions of the CPU. • To explain the basic function of the memory. • To describe a simple relationship between the parts of a computer.
3	Can name a sound file format. Can name a video file format.	• To name a sound file format, for example, .mp3. • To know that a sound file is stored on a digital device. • To name a video file format, for example, .mov. • To know that a video file is stored on a digital device.
4	Can explain the basic function of the hard disk.	• To explain the basic function of the hard disk. • To discuss that a hard disk stores data and form analogies with other data storage devices.
5	Can recognise common uses of technology outside of school, for example, at the zoo.	• To name common uses of technology within school. • To name common uses of technology outside of school. • To predict future uses of technology outside of school.
6	Can recognise common uses of technology outside of school, for example, in the local environment.	• To name common uses of technology outside of school. • To explain why technology is useful in the local environment.
Assess and review		• To assess the half-term's work.

Medium-term planning Spring 2: Ourselves

National Curriculum objective

Children should be taught to:
- use technology safely and respectfully, keeping personal information private; identify where to go for help and support when they have concerns about content or contact on the internet or other online technologies

W	Outcomes	Objectives
1	Can identify the traits of friends that they know and online friends. Can identify aspects of appropriate behaviour online.	• To list what makes a 'good' friend. • To identify how 'good' friends communicate through role-play. • To discuss methods of communication that are face-to-face. • To identify what to do when a friend upsets them – tell someone. • To discuss people who are not friends that they might meet online.
2	Can protect their identity online by not using their full name. Can protect their identity online by choosing an avatar.	• To discuss friends they meet in-person and online. • To know that an avatar is a picture to represent a person online. • To know that an avatar is a way of protecting identity online.
3	Can collaborate to create a story.	• To collaborate, face-to-face, to create a story. • To discuss non-verbal communication (for example, facial expressions).
4	Can collaborate online to create a story.	• To collaborate, using online tools, to create a story. • To discuss the differences between collaborating when face-to-face and when online.
5	Can explain how to collaborate respectfully.	• To discuss taking turns when collaborating on and offline. • To respect the views of others.
6	Can understand the need for clear communication, when collaborating online.	• To link to the learning on algorithms and precise instructions. • To explain how comments can be misunderstood when online compared with face-to-face.
Assess and review		• To assess the half-term's work.

■SCHOLASTIC

Medium-term planning Summer 1: Habitats

National Curriculum objective

Children should be taught to:
- use technology purposefully to create, organise, store, manipulate and retrieve digital content

W	Outcomes	Objectives
1	Can describe and use basic types of data. Can use technology to organise digital content.	• To identify the basic data types of image, video, audio and text. • To ask and answer simple questions about data in order to identify different minibeasts and their microhabitats. • To organise digital content in simple ways.
2	Can categorise data sets into groups. Can sort data according to specified criteria.	• To organise data into groups according to simple rules. • To sort the data according to specific attributes.
3	Can categorise data sets into groups. Can understand how a branching database works.	• To know what a branching database is and how it can be used. • To understand that a branching database can be created from a series of 'yes' and 'no' questions. • To be able to search a branching database to identify specific items and attributes. • To modify and extend a branching database.
4	Can categorise data sets into groups. Can create a simple branching database.	• To plan a simple branching database with accuracy. • To create a simple branching database. • To add additional questions and answers to a branching database. • To work with other to improve their work.
5	Can collect data using a tally sheet Can organise collected data in an effective way.	• To design a simple tally sheet for data collection. • To collect data from relevant people using a tally sheet. • To organise data in simple ways. • To draw simple initial conclusions from the data collected.
6	Can create digital block graphs to display data in graphical ways. Can analyse block graphs effectively.	• To understand that data can be displayed graphically and this can make data easier to interpret. • To know what a block graph is. • To display data they have collected using a simple block graph. • To draw conclusions from their data by analysing their block graph.
Assess and review		• To assess the half-term's work.

Medium-term planning Summer 2: Pirates

National Curriculum objective

Children should be taught to:
- use technology safely and respectfully, keeping personal information private; identify where to go for help and support when they have concerns about content or contact on the internet or other online technologies

W	Outcomes	Objectives
1	Can explain how to be respectful towards other people's information.	• To understand how to behave positively with others when face-to-face and online.
2	Can verbally communicate information with another child.	• To discuss methods of communication that are face-to-face. • To discuss methods of communication that are not face-to-face (for example, letters, postcards, email, *Facebook*). • To discuss friends they meet in-person and online.
3	Can use technology to communicate basic information.	• To understand how to behave positively with others when face-to-face and online.
4	Can explain where to go for help and support when they have concerns about content on digital devices.	• To identify what to do when a friend upsets them – tell someone. • To discuss people who are not friends, who they might meet online. • To form the link that online friends should behave kindly and if they upset you, tell someone.
5	Can explain where to go for help and support when they have concerns about content on the internet.	• To know who to go to for help and support when they have concerns about content on the internet.
6	Can explain where to go for help and support when they have concerns about content or contact on the internet.	• To begin to understand how to stay safe when online.
Assess and review		• To assess the half-term's work.

■SCHOLASTIC

Year 2 Background knowledge

In Year 2, the curriculum builds on and reinforces the knowledge acquired in Year 1. The children use new themes to practice and extend their problem solving skills, using computational thinking.

Algorithms and programming

The children should now recognise the word 'algorithm' and know that it means a sequence of instructions. In Year 2, greater accuracy in the steps towards problem solving is needed. Programming is introduced, where the computer is able to follow a set of instructions. The children practise programming, using simple on-screen devices to see that when an algorithm is not accurate, then the computer will not do as intended.

Computational thinking is developed through the creation of algorithms and then correcting errors. The process of removing errors is called 'debugging'. In Year 2, the children use logical reasoning to predict the behaviour of simple programs and debug them.

Children may have access to mobile devices or tablet computers in or outside of school. These will often contain games the children are familiar with. These games can be a good way to capture the interest of the children, by identifying the rules of the game and predicting the behaviour of the program, depending on the player's actions. Not only does this engage the children, it enables them to learn about the importance of identifying patterns and rules. For example, game score should increase, if a prize or token is collected. If the score reduces, then there might be a bug or error in the program. Programmers spend many hours ensuring games are bug-free. However, it can be noted that mobile apps include updates, which are written to fix bugs in the programs.

Data and information

In Year 2, children will be developing their analytical skills using data. The Key Stage 1 curriculum requires that they are not only organising and manipulating data, but that they can also create new data.

Also in Year 2, the children are required to store and retrieve digital content. This could involve saving their progress in a game and re-joining the game later. It is important that the children understand that this data is stored on the device (or online) to enable them to continue playing a game and not have to start from the beginning each time. They might also have used word-processing or paint programs, where they have 'saved' their work and reopened it, at a later date. Again, this concept of storing and retrieving digital content needs to be made explicit for them to understand the processes.

How computers work

In Year 2, children will be developing their awareness of technology inside school, such as the computer suite or tablet devices. Outside of school, they also need to recognise where computers are being used. They may have seen their people using credit cards in shops; this could lead them towards understanding that the card-reader is connected to another computer outside of the shop. The children may have heard phrases like 'the cloud', 'wifi' and the 'internet', but may not understand that computers are connecting to other computers to enable information to be transferred. Therefore, in Year 2, they need to be looking for devices that contain computers and begin to consider how they are connected. They can also use their imaginations to predict the future of computer-enabled devices.

Communication and e-safety

We encourage children to be aware of potential dangers when encountering people they have not met before. They should also be aware of these dangers as they begin to communicate online. In Year 2, you might limit such communication to known contacts within the class. However, it is important to reinforce the idea that they need to know who to go to for help and support when they have concerns about content or contact on the internet.

Year 3 Long-term planning

ALGORITHMS AND PROGRAMMING

The National Curriculum states that children should be taught to:

- debug programs that accomplish specific goals, including controlling or simulating physical systems; solve problems by decomposing them into smaller parts

- use sequence and repetition in programs

- use logical reasoning to explain how some simple algorithms work and to detect and correct errors in algorithms and programs

- Children should be debugging programs created in a visual programming language.

- To solve problems, children need to be decomposing them into smaller parts.

- Children can show and explain how algorithms can use selection (if) and repetition (loops) in programs.

- Continuing the theme from Year 2, children need to explain the need for accuracy of algorithms.

- As computers follow instructions blindly, they need more precise instructions than humans, in order to avoid errors.

- To know that programs are the sequences of precise instructions that control computers.

HOW COMPUTERS WORK

The National Curriculum states that children should be taught to:

- understand computer networks and the opportunities they offer for communication and collaboration

- use technology safely, respectfully and responsibly

- Children should explain and describe the key characteristics of basic computer architecture, building on their learning from Key Stage 1.

- They should explain why there are sometimes different operating systems and application software for the same hardware.

DATA AND INFORMATION

The National Curriculum states that children should be taught to:

- select, use and combine a variety of software to design and create a range of content that accomplishes given goals, including collecting and presenting data and information

- Data can have errors and so the children need to be 'data detectives' to spot them and aim to reduce them.

- By carefully questioning, children should predict how errors might affect the results and decisions based on the data.

COMMUNICATION AND E-SAFETY

The National Curriculum states that children should be taught to:

- use search technologies effectively

- use technology safely, respectfully and responsibly; identify a range of ways to report concerns about content and contact

- Developing the learning, the children should use search technologies to locate simple information.

- They need to use technology safely, respectfully and responsibly.

- In every year, they develop their skills in recognising acceptable or unacceptable behaviour and identify a range of ways to report concerns about content and contact.

Overview of progression in Year 3

Algorithms and programming

In Year 3, the children progress from creating and following algorithms to programming the computer. The firm foundations from the previous lessons will help them understand the need for accuracy.

'Decomposition' is a new focus in this year enabling programmers to break larger problems into smaller parts. This will be a crucial skill in the children's computing development.

Selection is introduced in the form of 'if' statements. Through verbal examples from the teacher, the children will come to realise that this conditional statement is often used in everyday life – e.g. *'If you do your homework, you can watch TV'*. The 'if' statement is often combined with repetition called a 'loop'. An example of this could be filling a glass of water – *'If the glass is full, then turn off the tap'*. What is actually happening while they are filling a glass is that they are constantly checking to see if it is full. *'Is the glass full? No, keep filling. Is the glass full? No, keep filling. Is the glass full? Yes, turn off the tap'*. They have 'looped' around to keep asking the question while it was 'No', until they received the answer 'Yes'.

The children are introduced to programming through the visual programming language, Scratch, developed by MIT (http:// scratch.mit.edu/). This allows them to develop their programming skills further and execute the algorithms they have designed.

Linking to the English curriculum, the focus is on children's comprehension. They are starting to recognise themes in what they are reading. The algorithms follow 'conventions' – similar to the structures of poems and stories. With non-fiction, children should know what information they need to look for before they begin and be clear about the task – again analogous to using algorithms and debugging them.

Data and information

The children reinforce their learning about algorithms and the need for accuracy in their data topic. They search through examples of data and a number of strategies are introduced to help them to reduce errors.

The children present their data using different software, to enable their peers to view and evaluate if they successfully cleaned up the 'dirty' data. They will also be developing their speaking and listening skills by providing constructive feedback. In mathematics, the children will be interpreting data presented in many contexts. Use of pictograms and bar charts supports the learning in their computing lessons.

How computers work

The children begin to think more about how computers communicate with each other. They are introduced to the concept of networks, forming analogies between friendship networks and computer networks. Through observation, the children identify wired and wireless networks used by computers in their school. They see there are other devices, such as printers, attached to the network. Finally, they collaborate using online tools, such as a wiki. They begin to see the benefits of networks of computers and how they can enable collaboration to occur.

Communication and e-safety

In the communication topic, the children link to the 'How computers work' topic and use the internet to perform simple searches. They develop the concepts of what are 'good' keywords using basic Boolean operators and how to approach reading the search results. Linking with the English curriculum, the children can compose writing about their research, for a range of real purposes and audiences.

For e-safety, the children build on the ideas of acceptable and unacceptable behaviour and how they can report concerns to someone they trust. Using examples of social media, such as Facebook, they explore their identities online. Using examples of different online behaviours, the children think through scenarios before applying the learning to their own situations.

Medium-term planning Autumn 1: Roald Dahl

National Curriculum objectives

Children should be taught to:
- understand computer networks including the internet; how they can provide multiple services, such as the world wide web; and the opportunities they offer for communication and collaboration
- use technology safely, respectfully and responsibly

W	Outcomes	Objectives
1	Can start to understand what a basic computer network is. Can discuss simply how computers communicate with each other.	• To understand the terminology 'computer network' (a group of two or more computers linked together). • To explain in simple terms how a network enables communication between computers.
2	Can describe how computers are networked in the room/school. Can create a simple diagram of the computer network.	• To recognise simple computer networks around them. • To sketch a simple diagram of a computer network. • To explain simply how the computers are communicating via the network.
3	Can discuss how other devices can be connected to the network. Can know that networks can be wired or wireless.	• To identify devices connected to a network including printers, mobile devices and laptops. • To add these to their simple network diagram. • To understand the simple concept that such devices can be wired to the network or be connected via a wireless network.
4	Can understand how computers offer opportunities for communication and collaboration. Can explain how computers can help others.	• To know that computers can enable communication in the classroom and beyond. • To discuss how computers have helped others in a variety of situations, such as remote schooling, developing countries etc. • To explain how computers can help people to communicate and collaborate.
5	Can use technology safely, respectfully and responsibly. Can use collaborative technology to collaborate with others.	• To know how they can collaborate with others in safe, respectful ways. • To use collaborative technology, such as a wiki, to communicate inside and outside school. • To use collaborative technology, such as a wiki, to collaborate within and beyond the classroom.
6	Can use technology to collaborate effectively with others. Can explain how collaborative technologies can be used to help others.	• To contribute to a document using collaborative technologies, such as a wiki. • To respond to others' work on a collaborative document, such as a wiki, in a supportive, constructive way. • To explain how using a wiki can help others to improve their ideas and think in new ways.
Assess and review		• To assess the half-term's work.

Medium-term planning Autumn 2: Robots

National Curriculum objectives

Children should be taught to:
- debug programs that accomplish specific goals, including controlling or simulating physical systems; solve problems by decomposing them into smaller parts
- use sequence and repetition in programs
- use logical reasoning to explain how some simple algorithms work and to detect and correct errors in algorithms and programs

W	Outcomes	Objectives
1	Can solve problems by decomposing them into smaller parts. Can use logical reasoning to be able to solve simple problems.	• To understand that by breaking down larger problems into smaller parts, a problem is easier to solve. • To use logic and persistence to solve a variety of different problems and puzzles. • To begin to understand that a problem can sometimes be solved in a number of different ways. • To be able to explain the steps taken to solve the problems and puzzles.
2	Can use sequencing and repetition when writing simple algorithms and explain how they work. Can use logical reasoning to include selection in simple algorithms and explain how they work.	• To be able to break down simple goals into their composite parts in order to create an accurate algorithm, for example how to make a drink or sandwich. • To create algorithms that achieve a specific goal using repeats where appropriate, for example, repeating the action of spreading butter. • To begin to understand how simple selection ('if' statements) can be used in algorithms. (For example, 'if the glass is full, then stop'.) • To be able to explain simply and verbally how their algorithms work.
3	Can use simple flowcharts to represent an algorithm. Can use logical reasoning to explain how sequencing, repetition and selection apply to algorithms.	• To recognise repetition and selection in algorithms in flowcharts. • To sequence flowcharts into the correct order to include repetition and selection. • To plan and create their own flowcharts using sequencing, repetition and selection. • To discuss the logical reasoning behind their flowchart.
4	Can explain how sequencing, repetition and selection work in algorithms. Can understand that computers need more precise instructions than humans.	• To prepare accurate algorithms for a human robot to achieve specific goals. • To follow instructions given verbally and visually, through flowcharts, by their peers. • To work cooperatively to detect and correct any errors in instructions. • To explain why robots, or computers, need precise instructions to carry out specific tasks.
5	Can create programs that accomplish simple specific goals, including controlling or simulating physical systems. Can solve problems by decomposing them into smaller parts.	• To create a disguise for their robot using a template. • To write algorithms for their robot to achieve a range of outcomes, such as sending it to a specific place. • To understand that their algorithm will be executed by a program within the robot. • To program the robot to make it perform a variety of creative tasks, such as making it dance.
6	Can detect and correct errors in simple algorithms and programs. Can use sequence and repetition in simple programs.	• To recognise and correct errors in their own and peers' algorithms. • To refine algorithms and programs previously written for their robots to include repetition and selection where appropriate. • To be able to explain verbally how and why they have included repetition and selection.
Assess and review		• To assess the half-term's work.

Medium-term planning Spring 1: Kings, queens and castles

National Curriculum objectives

Children should be taught to:
- use search technologies effectively
- use technology safely, respectfully and responsibly

W	Outcomes	Objectives
1	Can use search technologies effectively. Can locate specific information by using a search engine.	• To be able to use a child-friendly search engine accurately for simple research. • To understand how focussed search terms can return the most accurate results. • To find specific information about a particular topic (their chosen king, queen or castle). • To begin to understand which websites are likely to be the most trustworthy.
2	Can use search technologies effectively to search for a variety of media. Can use Boolean and advanced searching to narrow search results in simple ways.	• To be able to narrow searches by type (for example, image, video) and time (most recent). • To understand how basic Boolean searching (+, -) and basic advanced tools (for example, size of image) can be used to return more accurate results. • To use basic advanced searching techniques to research more accurate information about their chosen king, queen or castle.
3	Can identify key elements of an effective presentation. Can plan simple, effective designs on paper.	• To identify effective and poor presentations. • To devise a list of key elements of effective presentations. • To understand how to use images, text, colour and themes sparingly to enhance a presentation. • To understand why paper planning is an important part of the design process. • To create a simple storyboard for a five slide presentation on their chosen king, queen or castle.
4	Can create a simple five slide presentation. Can add simple text and images to their presentation.	• To use presentation software to create five slides. • To add appropriate and effective text and images to their presentation. • To give and receive effective feedback on the first drafts of presentations.
5	Can add other elements, such as colour and themes to their presentation as appropriate. Can add animation to their work if appropriate.	• To enhance their presentation with colour and themes/background as appropriate. • To add animations to their work as appropriate. • To discuss why such elements should be used sparingly. • To know how to print out their presentation in different views.
6	Can present their work to their peers.	• To know how to deliver an effective presentation to an audience. • To give their presentation to their peers. • To give and receive feedback on their presentations.
Assess and review		• To assess the half-term's work.

Medium-term planning Spring 2: Aliens

National Curriculum objectives

Children should be taught to:
- design, write and debug programs that accomplish specific goals, including controlling or simulating physical systems; solve problems by decomposing them into smaller parts
- use sequence and repetition in programs
- use logical reasoning to explain how some simple algorithms work and to detect and correct errors in algorithms and programs

W	Outcomes	Objectives
1	Can solve problems by decomposing them into smaller parts. Can use programming software to execute simple algorithms.	• To understand that *Scratch* is a software program that can execute algorithms. • To navigate around the *Scratch* interface. • To know how to add a sprite in *Scratch*. • To understand how to get a sprite to complete basic movements. • To understand how to add speech bubbles to sprites. • To explain to a beginner the interface of *Scratch* and how to get a sprite to move and speak.
2	Can use sequence and repetition in programs. Can use basic drawing tools to create simple artwork.	• To be able to paint a new sprite using basic drawing tools. • To create a short sequence of instructions to allow their sprite to perform multiple actions. • To use repeated actions when moving their sprite. • To be able to use simple repetition to make the algorithm more efficient.
3	Can use logical reasoning to explain how some simple algorithms work. Can use logical reasoning to detect and correct errors in algorithms and programs.	• To fulfil a series of simple challenges using *Scratch*. • To understand the process of debugging code within *Scratch*. • To work collaboratively with their peers to debug algorithms within *Scratch*. • To explain to others how they have debugged their code.
4	Can record sounds and create algorithms to play sounds. Can use basic drawing tools to create simple artwork.	• To record sounds using *Scratch*. • To add sounds to their code. • To use repetition and selection to achieve different outcomes with sounds in *Scratch*. • To be able to add backgrounds in *Scratch*.
5	Can plan a short joke animation in *Scratch*. Can create characters, backgrounds and sounds in *Scratch*.	• To plan and create a short joke animation using a template. • To create their own sprites in *Scratch* for their joke. • To add a background in *Scratch* for their joke. • To create their own sounds to add to their joke.
6	Can create and debug simple algorithms that accomplish specific goals.	• To create algorithms for their joke animation. • To program their algorithms into *Scratch*. • To test and debug their algorithms. • To give and receive constructive feedback. • To use logical reasoning to explain how the algorithms within their joke work.
Assess and review		• To assess the half-term's work.

Medium-term planning Summer 1: Chocolate

YEAR 3

National Curriculum objective

Children should be taught to:
- select, use and combine a variety of software to design and create a range of content that accomplishes given goals, including collecting and presenting data and information

W	Outcomes	Objectives
1	Can collect data using a tally sheet. Can organise collected data in an effective way.	• To design a simple tally sheet for data collection. • To collect data from relevant people (about chocolate preferences) using a tally sheet. • To organise data in simple ways. • To represent data pictorially using chocolate bar wrappers. • To draw simple initial conclusions from the data collected.
2	Can analyse simple 'dirty' data to check for errors. Can explain why errors can occur when collecting data. Can explain reasons for correcting errors in simple data.	• To look at simple 'dirty' data and identify obvious errors. • To explain how errors can occur when collecting data. • To explain the reasons why data was identified as being incorrect (in relation to the data set).
3	Can analyse simple block graphs to check for errors. Can explain reasons for correcting errors in simple block graphs.	• To look at simple block graphs and identify obvious errors. • To explain how errors can occur when collecting data. • To explain the reasons why data was identified as being incorrect (in a block graph).
4	Can collect data using software. Can organise collected data in an effective way. Can create simple graphs using software.	• To collect data about chocolate using software to collate the responses. • To use software to organise the data. • To create simple graphs using the software. • To demonstrate that they have checked for errors.
5	Can work collaboratively with peers on a project. Can collaborate to create a presentation. Can contribute information for a presentation, from gathered data. Can combine different software to create a presentation.	• To learn to work on projects with their peers cooperatively. • To identify how larger tasks can be broken down into smaller tasks (decomposition) and distributed throughout the group to achieve a goal. • To identify an area to research on the process of making chocolate bars, from bean to bar. • To collect relevant information to contribute to a presentation. • To use more than one piece of software to create the presentation.
6	Can deliver a presentation to their peers. Can give and receive constructive feedback on presentations.	• To deliver a chocolate presentation to their peers in an effective way. • To receive and give feedback in the form of two stars and a wish, or similar, from their peers. • To explain verbally or in simple written form as appropriate how they would improve their approach to a similar project in the future.
Assess and review		• To assess the half-term's work.

Medium-term planning Summer 2: Superheroes

National Curriculum objectives

Children should be taught to:
- use search technologies effectively
- use technology safely, respectfully and responsibly; recognise acceptable/unacceptable behaviour; identify a range of ways to report concerns about content and contact

W	Outcomes	Objectives
1	Can use technology safely, respectfully and responsibly. Can recognise acceptable/unacceptable behaviour.	• To understand what is meant by the term 'social media'. • To know the main social media channels. • To discuss the main, age appropriate, potential issues surrounding social media. • To start to understand how social media can be a positive source of communication.
2	Can use social media safely, respectfully and responsibly. Can identify a range of ways to report concerns about content and contact.	• To learn what *Facebook* is. • To know how *Facebook* is used by individuals and organisations. • To understand *Facebook* age limits and the reasons behind the age limits. • To understand what information and media can be safely shared on *Facebook* and what is best kept private.
3	Can use search technologies effectively. Can save and retrieve documents effectively.	• To use basic advanced searching techniques to research information about their chosen superhero. • To be able to narrow searches by type (for example, image, video) and time (most recent). • To use basic Boolean searching (+, -) and basic advanced tools (for example, size of image) to return more accurate results. • To save text information in text editing software for inclusion in their superhero *Facebook* page. • To save images in a folder for use in their superhero *Facebook* page.
4	Can plan on paper an effective superhero Facebook page. Can combine different media to create an effective social media page.	• To create a paper design for a superhero *Facebook* page. • To combine images, text and other media in a visually effective way. • To include relevant content that is appropriate to share.
5	Can use a template to create an effective superhero *Facebook* page.	• To open a saved template in a shared area. • To save a saved template in their own area. • To insert saved images into their superhero *Facebook* page. • To add suitable text to their superhero *Facebook* page. • To add other media as appropriate to their superhero *Facebook* page.
6	Can explain why they have included and excluded information from their Facebook page. Can explain how to use social media safely, respectfully and responsibly.	• To discuss their superhero *Facebook* page and demonstrate how they have created it. • To explain verbally why they have included certain content and left out other information. • To create top five tips on using *Facebook*. • To discuss how their learning on *Facebook* can be applied across other social media.
Assess and review		• To assess the half-term's work.

Year 3 Background knowledge

Algorithms and programming

To further develop the children's experience in computational thinking in Year 3 they begin to focus on 'decomposition' – breaking larger problems into smaller ones.

Decomposition

When children have a task to do, such as, getting dressed, they know that they cannot put on every piece of clothing at exactly the same time, so they need to break this 'problem' into smaller parts. However, they do not realise that is what they are doing; so through discussion the teacher needs to get them thinking about how they already use decomposition in this way. Linking to programming, they can look at a simple example and see how it is broken down into smaller instructions.

The children are introduced to a visual programming language, for example, *Scratch*, developed by the Massachusetts Institute of Technology (http://scratch.mit.edu/). This represents the instructions as a 'visual' block, which can be combined with other instruction blocks to execute a program. Below are some examples of the types of instruction:

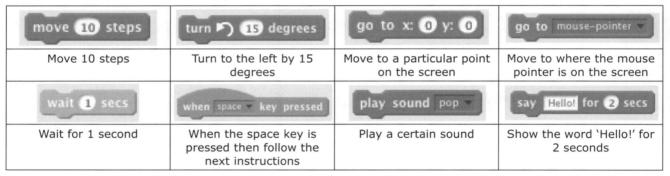

move 10 steps	turn ↺ 15 degrees	go to x: 0 y: 0	go to mouse-pointer ▼
Move 10 steps	Turn to the left by 15 degrees	Move to a particular point on the screen	Move to where the mouse pointer is on the screen
wait 1 secs	when space ▼ key pressed	play sound pop ▼	say Hello! for 2 secs
Wait for 1 second	When the space key is pressed then follow the next instructions	Play a certain sound	Show the word 'Hello!' for 2 seconds

Debugging

The children look at programs and try to identify errors. This is an important skill to develop.

Selection and repetition

An example of selection is an 'If' statement. The children may be familiar with conditional statements, for example, 'If you press the doorbell button, then the bell will ring'. The 'if' statement is conditional on something happening or a decision being made.

Repetition is displayed as a 'loop' statement; the program will continue to loop around the same point, unless there is something to 'break' that continuous loop. This is when an 'if' statement could be combined with a loop. A simple example is, children on a long car journey saying, 'Are we there yet?' over and over until they arrive. Imagine the journey begins: *'If we have arrived at the destination, then the children can stop asking 'Are we there yet? If we have not arrived then continue to check if we have arrived.'*

Flowcharts

In Year 3, the children will be introduced to simple flowcharts, to represent algorithms. Using the car journey example::

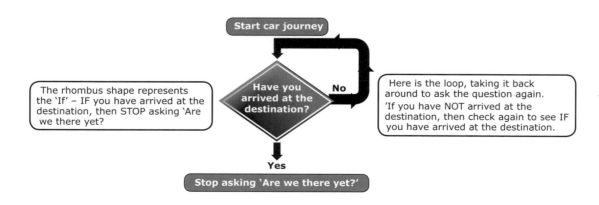

■SCHOLASTIC

Year 4 Long-term planning

ALGORITHMS AND PROGRAMMING

The National Curriculum states that children should be taught to:

- write and debug programs that accomplish specific goals, including controlling or simulating physical systems; solve problems by decomposing them into smaller parts

- use sequence, selection, and repetition in programs; work with variables

- use logical reasoning to explain how some simple algorithms work and to detect and correct errors in algorithms and programs

---

- At this stage, the children should be writing and debugging programs using a visual programming language.

- The focus for this year is on the children working with programs within programs.

- Children should be decomposing problems into smaller parts.

- Children should be able to explain and show how to use sequence, selection and repetition in programs.

- To test a hypothesis, children should show how to use programs to simulate environments.

- Children can distinguish between an algorithm and the program that implements that algorithm.

HOW COMPUTERS WORK

The National Curriculum states that children should be taught to:

- understand computer networks and the opportunities they offer for communication and collaboration

- use technology safely, respectfully and responsibly

- Through observations and experience of different computers in and out of school, the children can explain why there are sometimes different operating systems and application software for the same hardware.

- There are many possibilities for collaboration online using the internet, so the children need to be made aware of how they can communicate and work together.

DATA AND INFORMATION

The National Curriculum states that children should be taught to:

- select, use and combine a variety of software (including internet services) to create a range of content that accomplishes given goals, including collecting and presenting data and information

---

- The children will explain the importance of human-computer interface design, for example, how a website is designed to help the user navigate the pages.

- Children will explain and used common troubleshooting techniques to find errors in data.

COMMUNICATION AND E-SAFETY

The National Curriculum states that children should be taught to:

- use search technologies effectively and be discerning in evaluating digital content

- use technology safely, respectfully and responsibly; recognise acceptable/unacceptable behaviour; identify a range of ways to report concerns about content and contact

---

- Though children use search technologies often to find information, they will learn to be more accurate in their choice of keywords.

- Once information has been located, the children will evaluate it for relevance and appropriateness.

- In each year, the children need to develop their use of technology to be safe, respectful and responsible online.

- The children will be developing skills to recognise acceptable or unacceptable behaviour of others.

- Building on the prior learning, children should know a range of ways to report concerns about content and contact.

Overview of progression in Year 4

Algorithms and programming

In Year 4, children will progress by writing their own programs to achieve specific goals. Using the visual programming language, Scratch, they will create an interactive-quiz program based on a science fiction theme, debugging their program as they create it to correct any errors. They will also need to explain the difference between the algorithm and the program that implements it.

A new concept for Year 4 children will be the introduction of 'variables', which are ways of storing values in a container. For example, when scoring a goal in a game, at the start of a game, a player has zero goals, so the variable called 'Number of Goals' can be given the value of '0'. This can change so that if the player scores a goal, then the container holding the value of 'Number of Goals' is set to '1' and so on. The children need to be secure in their place value of numbers, to be able to manipulate the variables confidently.

The children will plan their programs using increasing complexity from Year 3. They will use selection commands, such as, 'If' statements and loops, to check the status of a particular statement. These skills build upon the previous work on algorithms and programming.

To develop the use of logic, the children will predict the outcome of their program. They will be able to 'see what happens', comparing it with what they would have expected to happen. This links to the English curriculum through reading stories and predicting the outcome based on a pattern, such as a story arc. They will be developing their comprehension skills in understanding the problem and also their composition skills in documenting their findings. Linking to maths, the children will be improving their problem solving strategies, using trial and improvement.

Data and information

In Year 4, the children consider different representations of data. Looking at pictograms and graphs they recognise that the data tells a story. They can create simple timelines to represent events through history. The children can create questionnaires and by using simple, web-based collaboration tools, they can gather required information. Using their knowledge from Year 3, they can search through the results and identify any errors in the data. In all of the activities, the children need to consider their audience and how to present the information appropriately.

In the English curriculum, they are learning conventions of different types of writing. Forming unambiguous questions that can be answered clearly is an important skill.

How computers work

During the previous years, the children have been developing their knowledge of computer hardware. The concept that computers can be connected using networks was also introduced. In Year 4, the focus is on operating systems and software. Different software tools can perform different roles and have different functions. It is important for the children to observe and evaluate the software they encounter, thinking about its purpose and if it is the correct tool for the required activity. The children may be familiar with the 'App store' or 'Google Play' where different applications can be purchased and downloaded. These apps, generally, perform one or two simple tasks. By contrast, software on the PC or Mac computer can be complex, in order to carry out a wide range of tasks. The children design a 'Sci-fi' app for the future, thinking about its appropriateness for purpose

Communication and e-safety

In Year 4, the children will use online tools to communicate not only with their friends in the classroom, but beyond that to children in other schools and in other countries. They create a simple blog post to share information. This is closely linked to the e-safety learning on behaving respectfully online, by giving kind, specific and helpful feedback through comments.

Medium-term planning Autumn 1: Myths and legends

National Curriculum objective

Children should be taught to:
• use search technologies effectively and be discerning in evaluating digital content

W	Outcomes	Objectives
1	Can give a simple definition of a myth and legend. Can use search technologies to locate and evaluate information.	• To define a myth and legend. • To retell a simple myth and legend. • To identify the main steps in a story. • To use a search engine to locate basic information. • To know there are many different search engines. • To use at least two search engines. • To evaluate located information using given simple criteria.
2	Can define a spam email or message. Can explain what to do when receiving a spam email or message.	• To know a spam email or message can be misleading. • To give a simple definition of a spam message. • To make analogies with April Fool hoaxes and spam messages. • To know that some spam messages may be dangerous. • To begin to recognise the features of a spam message. • To know what to do if they suspect a message to be spam.
3	Can explain that websites may not contain truthful information. Can read myths and legends and identify information and discuss if it is truthful.	• To know that websites may not contain truthful information. • To make analogies with fake stories in books and misleading websites. • To read myths and legends and identify information that may or may not be truthful.
4	Can create a 'fake' website based on a myth, using different software. Can evaluate peers' websites, using given criteria.	• To create a 'fake' website based on a myth. • To combine software tools to create the design of a website. • To evaluate other children's websites, using given criteria.
5	Can search for images of fictional inventions. Can evaluate the images to state whether they are truthful.	• To search for fictional inventions (for example, Boilerplate robot, Chindogu). • To describe the features of a trustworthy website. • To evaluate images to state whether they are truthful and justify decisions.
6	Can explain that websites may not contain truthful information or may have a bias. Can identify the general type of a website, based on the address.	• To know that websites may contain misleading information. • To explain what bias means. • To know and explain that websites may contain bias. • To recognise types of organisations by their website address.
Assess and review		• To assess the half-term's work.

Medium-term planning Autumn 2: Science fiction

National Curriculum objectives

Children should be taught to:
- understand computer networks and the opportunities they offer for communication and collaboration

W	Outcomes	Objectives
1	Can give examples of computers present inside and outside of school. Can understand why computers are used. Can identify examples of physical, wireless and mobile networks and know the difference between them. Can name different operating systems. Can understand the main functions of the operating system.	• To name examples of computers present inside and outside the school. • To describe the function of the computers and why they are used. • To give examples of physical, wireless and mobile networks and describe the difference between them. • To name different operating systems. • To describe the main functions of an operating system.
2	Can explain why different computers might use different operating systems for the same hardware. Can identify software on a computer and describe its function. Can explain why different pieces of software may be used for different functions.	• To use a Sci-fi theme to describe different operating systems for the same hardware. • To explain why different computers use different operating systems. • To identify software on a computer. • To describe how different software can have different functions.
3	Can describe and define the functions of an 'app' for a mobile phone or tablet computer. Can explain that app stores are used to download an app onto a device. Can create a model tablet or mobile phone and identify the main features.	• To describe an app and its functions. • To describe the mobile technology the children may use, for example, mobile phones or tablet devices. • To explain how people may use apps everyday for specific tasks. • To know that apps can be downloaded from an app store. • To create a model tablet or mobile phone and identify its main features.
4	Can design an app for a fictional Sci-fi story Can describe and define the functions of an 'app' for a mobile phone or tablet computer. Can add a fictional app to a model mobile phone or tablet device.	• To discuss what new things might be around in the future. • To discuss what would the children like to see in the future. • To imagine the impact of new technologies on their lives. • To design an app for a Sci-fi story • To invent the functions for a future Sci-fi app. • To add the imaginary app to their mobile device model.
5	Can use a collaborative web tool to compose a newspaper report. Can collaborate on one document with other pupils, using an online tool.	• To look at example newspaper reports and analyse them to highlight direct speech, the use of captions and text layout. • To plan an imaginary Sci-fi newspaper article (using 'Who, what, why, when and how'). • To write an imaginary Sci-fi newspaper article using an online tool. • To collaborate on one document with other pupils, using an online tool.
6	Can present to an audience to describe an app and its function. Can explain how more than one pupil collaborated using an online tool. Can record progress of learning, using an online tool.	• To present to an audience to describe the Sci-fi app • To describe the function of the Sci-fi app • To explain how more than pupil can collaborate on one document. • To demonstrate how to use a collaborative tool. • To use a collaborative tool to demonstrate the class' progress of learning over the topic.
Assess and review		• To assess the half-term's work.

Medium-term planning Spring 1: Dragons

National Curriculum objectives

Children should be taught to:
- write and debug programs that accomplish specific goals, including controlling or simulating physical systems; solve problems by decomposing them into smaller parts
- use sequence, selection and repetition in programs; work with variables
- use logical reasoning to explain how some simple algorithms work and to detect and correct errors in algorithms and programs

W	Outcomes	Objectives
1	Can understand what makes a good animation. Can evaluate an animated game based on given criteria.	• To understand what an animation is. • To identify what makes an effective animation. • To establish their own criteria for effective animations. • To evaluate an animation, using their own criteria. • To identify what elements they can include in their own short animation to ensure it is effective.
2	Can plan a simple animation using a template. Can explain why their animation will be effective.	• To understand why planning is important. • To brainstorm ideas for their own animation and develop one. • To give and receive feedback to their peers. • To understand what a storyboard is. • To plan a simple animation using a given paper storyboard template. • To check they have included identified elements to ensure their animation is effective and explain how they have done so.
3	Can plan what assets to use within their animation. Can use multimedia tools to create effective assets for their animations.	• To identify the assets needed for their animation. • To use built-in sounds and sprites for their animation as appropriate. • To understand the importance of naming assets carefully within their animation. • To use basic drawing tools to create multiple sprites and backgrounds for their animation. • To record appropriate sounds for their animation.
4	Can plan algorithms to achieve predicted outcomes. Can use repetition (loops) and selection where appropriate.	• To use logical thinking to plan appropriate algorithms for their animation. • To use decomposition to break down algorithms into smaller parts. • To identify and use selection and repetition as appropriate within their algorithms. • To explain their algorithms verbally to their peers. • To give and receive feedback. • To debug their algorithms as appropriate after feedback. • To start to implement their algorithms using the Scratch programming language.
5	Can implement algorithms using a suitable program. Can use repetition (loops) and selection where appropriate.	• To implement their algorithms using the *Scratch* programming language. • To use selection and repetition as appropriate within their program. • To work collaboratively with their peers to test and debug programs. • To give and receive constructive feedback.
6	Can work collaboratively to debug algorithms and programs to achieve specific goals. Can evaluate their work in simple ways.	• To add simple comments to a program. • To explain why adding comments can help the programmer. • To explain how comments can help other people viewing a program. • To evaluate the program of an animated game.
Assess and review		• To assess the half-term's work.

Medium-term planning Spring 2: Norman's Bayeux Tapestry

National Curriculum objective

Children should be taught to:
- select, use and combine a variety of software (including internet services) to create a range of content that accomplishes given goals, including collecting and presenting data and information

W	Outcomes	Objectives
1	Can identify and interpret simple pictograms and graphs. Can explain that data can tell a story.	• To identify simple pictograms and graphs. • To interpret simple pictograms and graphs. • To explain that data tells a story. • To create paper-based pictograms and living graphs to describe well-known stories.
2	Can identify a timeline. Can interpret simple timelines. Can create simple timelines using software.	• To identify a timeline. • To interpret simple timelines (for example, major historical events in their life times). • To create simple timelines using paper-based tools. • To explain what the Bayeux Tapestry is and why it is important.
3	Can create a timeline for a specific purpose. Can research online to locate historical information for a timeline. Can check for errors in information.	• To create simple timelines (for example, of the children's own lives) using software or online tools. • To research online to locate historical information. • To check for errors in the created timelines.
4	Can combine different media to create interactive timelines. Can explain the importance of human-computer interface design.	• To research to collect different media for use in a timeline. • To evaluate the located media, using given criteria. • To describe the buttons and menus of the software and how they are adapted for the user. • To explain the importance of human-computer interface design.
5	Can present information to their peers. Can evaluate presentations, using given criteria.	• To present information, in the form of a timeline, to their peers. • To evaluate presentations, using given criteria. • To create new evaluation criteria, as a group or class.
6	Can describe different formats for presenting data. Can justify the format of presentation for a specific purpose.	• To describe different formats for presenting data. • To describe why certain formats are more suitable than others for particular data. • To justify the choice of format of presentation of data, for a specific purpose.
Assess and review		• To assess the half-term's work.

Medium-term planning Summer 1: Jacqueline Wilson

National Curriculum objective

Children should be taught to:
- use technology safely, respectfully and responsibly
- select, use and combine a variety of software (including internet services) on a range of digital devices to design and create a range of programs, systems and content that accomplish given goals, including collecting, analysing, evaluating and presenting data and information

W	Outcomes	Objectives
1	Can discuss online identities, including profiles. Can describe how to search for information about personalities and discuss the validity of the information.	• To identify characters from fictional books. • To describe characters from fictional books; to begin to develop profiles. • To identify personalities from real life and locate information about them, using search tools. • To describe the validity of the information located.
2	Can create a profile for a character in a book, based on information located. Can create a profile for a current celebrity, based on information located.	• To decide the type of information required in a profile of a person. • To create a profile for a fictional character in a book based on the information located.
3	Can create a user guide for peers, for locating digital content and how to evaluate it. Can use different software and understand different hardware may have different software (for example, tablet operating systems and apps).	• To describe locating information and evaluating it, in the form of a user guide for their peers. • To proofread materials before sharing with others. • To use a given checklist to check information before sharing it. • To name different software used on different hardware. • To explain why different hardware may use different software.
4	Can collaborate face-to-face to plan a new story. Can collaborate online to plan a new story. Can compare the processes of collaborating face-to-face and online.	• To collaborate to create a new story, in-person and face-to-face. • To collaborate using online tools to plan and create a new story. • To compare the writing processes of online and in-person collaboration and describe the advantages and disadvantages. • To correct errors using software tools, such as, spell checking.
5	Can explain why there are different application software for different purposes. Can create a simple blog using online tools.	• To name different application software and describe its functions. • To explain why different application software is used for different purposes. • To explain the function of a blog. • To create a simple blog.
6	Can give positive and supportive comments, using a blog. Can evaluate the information given within a blog.	• To read and review blog comments, using given criteria. • To respond to a blog post, giving positive and supportive comments. • To evaluate blogs for the quality of information shared, using given criteria.
Assess and review		• To assess the half-term's work.

Medium-term planning Summer 2: Rainforest

National Curriculum objectives

Children should be taught to:
- write and debug programs that accomplish specific goals, including controlling or simulating physical systems; solve problems by decomposing them into smaller parts
- use sequence, selection, and repetition in programs; work with variables
- use logical reasoning to explain how some simple algorithms work and to detect and correct errors in algorithms and programs
- use search technologies effectively and be discerning in evaluating digital content
- use technology safely, respectfully and responsibly; recognise acceptable/unacceptable behaviour; identify a range of ways to report concerns about content and contact.

W	Outcomes	Objectives
1	Can use search technologies to locate and evaluate information. Can explain that websites may not contain truthful information.	• To use a search engine to locate basic information. • To know there are many different search engines. • To use at least two search engines. • To evaluate located information using given simple criteria. • To know that websites may not contain truthful information.
2	Can plan a simple quiz based on a given topic. Can search for images and content using appropriate search words and determine the trustworthiness of content.	• To use search engines to locate images, using appropriate search terms (for example, 'of the rainforest'). • To evaluate the images to state whether they are truthful or may contain bias.
3	Can create a simple quiz using a visual programming language. Can solve problems by decomposing them into smaller parts.	• To create an animation or quiz using a visual programming language. • To modify an animation or quiz to create a simple game using keyboard keys for input. • To decompose a problem into smaller parts. • To plan and explain an algorithm using flowcharts. • To evaluate an animated game or quiz, using given criteria.
4	Can use selection and repetition within a program. Can debug a program.	• To modify an animated game or quiz to include more than one variable. • To explain how algorithms can use sequence, selection and repetition in programs. • To modify an expression in a program (for example, to change the score in a game or answer to a quiz question). • To work with variables within programs. • To test hypotheses, by using programs to simulate environments. • To distinguish between an algorithm and the program that implements the algorithm.
5	Can understand the use of variables. Can declare and assign variables within a program.	• To add simple comments to a flowchart and a program. • To explain why adding comments can help the programmer. • To explain how comments can help other people viewing a program. • To evaluate the program of an animated game.
6	Can evaluate their own and others' work using given criteria. Can explain how they have used selection, repetition and variables in their work.	• To present to their peers, considering the main features of their game or quiz. • To evaluate a presentation, using given criteria.
Assess and review		• To assess the half-term's work.

Year 4 Background knowledge

Algorithms and programming

In Year 4, the children are beginning to use variables. Working with variables is key in their development of programs. A variable is a label for a value, which is stored in the computer's memory. For example, in a game, it could be the number of lives a player has. If they have 3 lives at the start the 'Number of lives' variable would contain '3'. When they lose a life a new value of '2' must be placed in that container.

The children's knowledge of numbers in their maths lessons, can help them in their programming. By saying the problem aloud, they can refine it. For example: "The player's score needs to go up by 1000", "So, we need to get the current score and add 1000 to it." This leads to creating an equation, score = score + 1000. Once the children have seen examples of this type of equation, they should be able to apply to different situations.

In *Scratch*, the user can create new variables, for example,

Then select 'Make a variable':

Give the variable the name 'score', this is called 'defining a variable' (giving it a name).

This then creates a set of blocks that can be used to change the score within the program.

Variables can be given values at the start of a program, in the example 'set score to 0' could be changed to a large number. The score could decrease by 100 every time the player touches an enemy character or gets an answer incorrect in a quiz (for example, using 'change score by -100).

Year 5 Long-term planning

ALGORITHMS AND PROGRAMMING

The National Curriculum states that children should be taught to:

- design, write and debug programs that accomplish specific goals, including controlling or simulating physical systems; solve problems by decomposing them into smaller parts

- use sequence, selection, and repetition in programs; work with variables and various forms of input and output

- use logical reasoning to explain how some simple algorithms work and to detect and correct errors in algorithms and programs

---

- Progressing from the previous learning, children should design, write and debug programs in multiple programming languages (visual or text-based).

- The essential skills of solving problems by decomposing them into smaller parts should continue to develop.

- Developing vocabulary and speaking and listening skills, in addition to programming skills, the children should explain and show how algorithms can use sequence, selection and repetition in programs.

- Children should develop their use of variables and how they work with various forms of input and output.

- In order to increase efficiency, the children need to be able to explain and show how programs can use procedures or subroutines within a program.

- Good planning can help in their programming, so children need to explain and show how programs can be planned, tested, corrected and documented.

- To enable the children to share their understanding of programming, they need to annotate programs with simple comments.

HOW COMPUTERS WORK

The National Curriculum states that children should be taught to:

- understand computer networks including the internet; how they can provide multiple services, such as the World Wide Web; and the opportunities they offer for communication and collaboration

- use technology safely, respectfully and responsibly

- Children need to explain to what they understand by the term 'World Wide Web'. They also need to describe the term 'the internet'. They need to be able to describe the difference between them.

- As the children develop their understanding of how computers work, they should outline how data are transported on the internet, including packets and the concept of a protocol.

DATA AND INFORMATION

The National Curriculum states that children should be taught to:

- select, use and combine a variety of software (including internet services) on a range of digital devices to design and create a range of programs, systems and content that accomplish given goals, including collecting, evaluating and presenting data and information

---

- Building on the experience in Year 4, the children should be more critical in their explanations of the importance of human-computer interface design.

- In Year 5, the binary number system is introduced to support learning about networks. They should be able to name and explain how a number can be represented in binary.

- The children can explain how the same information can be represented in a computer in a variety of ways.

- When thinking about information, the children need to explain safety and security, related to technology.

COMMUNICATION AND E-SAFETY

The National Curriculum states that children should be taught to:

- use search technologies effectively and be discerning in evaluating digital content

- use technology safely, respectfully and responsibly; recognise acceptable/unacceptable behaviour; identify a range of ways to report concerns about content and contact

---

- Building on the previous years' learning, the children use search technologies effectively and become discerning in evaluating the located information.

Overview of progression in Year 5

Algorithms and programming

In Year 5, children really progress in problem solving and program writing. They spend longer designing and planning programs and use decomposition to reduce larger problems into smaller parts.

The children continue to build on their understanding of selection and repetition in their programs.

Using a maze game theme, the children identify the features of maze games and establish their criteria for what makes a 'good' game. They progress by adding multiple variables, to make the game more interesting for the player. These variables can be for scores, timers and numbers of lives. They also, collaboratively debug their code, in addition to debugging by themselves.

Linking with the English curriculum, the children focus on documenting their programs. This can be through adding comments into the program itself. These comments are useful to have an insight into the programmer's thoughts. Another method is to capture images of the program and add labels to explain the function of each part. They can also think aloud to generate ideas, draft their comments and re-read to check that their meaning is clear.

Data and information

In Year 5, the children use a wider range of tools, software and internet services to collect and present data. They consider the importance of the human to computer interface, by reviewing and designing different questionnaire forms. They describe how 'useable' an interface is and how it could be improved.

To present data, the children use software and online 'infographic' tools to convey a specific purpose. This links with the English curriculum by focusing on presenting to different audiences and evaluating fact versus opinion. Linking to the maths curriculum, they begin to decide which representations of data are most appropriate and can justify their answers.

To explain how computers communicate, the binary number system is introduced in Year 5. It supports the maths curriculum, reinforcing place value and number systems.

How computers work

In Year 5, the children learn more about the World Wide Web and the internet. It is important that they understand that the internet is a massive network of computers joined together around the world. They learn how the information is transported, beginning with activities to send and receive messages. The analogy is continued by talking about 'packets' of information being sent and received by computers. The children will further progress to understand that a protocol helps to organise the data so that the computers can understand each other. Finally, the children are introduced to the binary number system. The computer data is in the form of the binary code, so the children learn how the ones and zeros are used to form this information.

Communication and e-safety

In Year 5, the children focus on developing their searching skills on the World Wide Web and being more discerning in evaluating the content they find. The children need to consider where there may be bias in the search rankings or where certain advertisers have promoted their site towards the top of the results.

For e-safety, children consider automatic filtering of web content and whether this can affect safety online. They develop their awareness of how people can use technology to deceive others and balance this with the potential to collaborate with people in different countries.

Medium-term planning Autumn 1: King Arthur

National Curriculum objectives

Children should be taught to:
- design, write and debug programs that accomplish specific goals, including controlling or simulating physical systems; solve problems by decomposing them into smaller parts
- use sequence, selection, and repetition in programs; work with variables and various forms of input and output
- use logical reasoning to explain how some simple algorithms work and to detect and correct errors in algorithms and programs

W	Outcomes	Objectives
1	Can use logical reasoning to solve a variety of puzzles. Can recognise and extend patterns.	• To develop problem solving skills by solving different puzzles. • To decompose larger problems into smaller ones. • To use logical reasoning to recognise and extend image and number patterns.
2	Can use logical reasoning and decomposition to break codes. Can develop own code breaking activities for peers.	• To use logical reasoning to solve code problems. • To be able to use decomposition to break larger code problems into smaller ones. • To understand techniques that can be used to design and break codes. • To create own codes for others to solve.
3	Can create algorithms to draw simple shapes. Can use sequences of loops (repetition) to create efficient algorithms.	• To decompose the task of drawing a shape into sub-tasks. • To write algorithms for drawing simple shapes. • To use loops (repetition) to design efficient algorithms. • To test and debug their algorithms as necessary. • To explain how they have used loops to make their algorithm efficient.
4	Can write a program to execute their algorithm to draw simple shapes. Can explain how their program is using loops.	• To use a program to implement their designed algorithms. • To work collaboratively to debug their algorithms as necessary. • To explain how the program is executing their algorithm and using loops efficiently.
5	Can understand why comments are used in computer programs. Can annotate a program with simple comments.	• To know that comments can be added to a program. • To annotate a program with simple comments. • To work collaboratively to ensure comments are clear and unambiguous. • To be able to explain why comments are useful when writing programs.
6	Can understand the use of conditions and two way selection when writing simple algorithms and programs. Can use conditions and two-way selection in algorithms and programs.	• To understand how and why conditions and two-way selection are used in algorithms and programs. • To design, write and test a program that uses conditions and two-way selection. • To debug their program as necessary. • To annotate their program with simple comments. • To explain how their program uses conditions and two-way selection.
Assess and review		• To assess the half-term's work.

Medium-term planning Autumn 2: The Railway Children

National Curriculum objectives

Children should be taught to:
- understand computer networks including the internet; how they can provide multiple services, such as the World Wide Web; and the opportunities they offer for communication and collaboration
- use technology safely, respectfully and responsibly

W	Outcomes	Objectives
1	Can explain what the World Wide Web and the internet are and explain the difference. Can use analogies of train tracks and trains to describe the internet.	• To describe the internet in terms of a global network. • To describe the World Wide Web and how users connect. • To explain the difference between the World Wide Web and the internet. • To use analogies to describe networks, including the internet (for example, using train track networks).
2	Can send and receive messages using different methods. Can use the paper-chase analogy (example in *The Railway Children*) to show how web pages can be broken into smaller packets of data.	• To send and receive messages using paper. • To send and receive messages using online tools. • To compare sending and receiving messages using physical methods and online tools. • To use an analogy to describe how data can be broken into packets of data (for example, the paper chase sequence in *The Railway Children*).
3	Can describe how data are transported on the internet, including packets and the notion of a protocol. Can create a simple model to describe how the web pages are formed from packets.	• To describe how packets of data can be transported on the internet. • To describe how data can be transported using a protocol to organise them. • To create a simple model to describe how web pages are formed from packets.
4	Can use the binary number system to count to ten. Can explain that computers communicate using binary code.	• To use the binary number system to count to ten. • To know that computers use binary code to communicate. • To describe how the telegraph was used in the railway system to send messages via Morse code and how computers can send messages using binary code.
5	Know that a byte is a unit of digital information. Can explain that large volumes of data can be described using terms, such as, kilobytes, megabytes and gigabytes. Can identify examples of digital information in everyday life.	• To know that a byte is a collection of digital information. • To explain that large volumes of data can be given a prefix, such as, kilobytes, megabytes, gigabytes and larger. • To recognise examples of kilobytes, megabytes, gigabytes, in everyday life.
6	Can discuss the health and safety aspects of using technology.	• To retell a story and describe how the development of technology has benefitted everyday life (for example, the technological improvements in *The Railway Children* and since that period). • To discuss how technology in modern life can affect our health in both positive and negative ways. • To use technology safely and responsibly.
Assess and review		• To assess the half-term's work.

Medium-term planning Spring 1: China and India

National Curriculum objectives

Children should be taught to:
- use search technologies effectively and be discerning in evaluating digital content
- use technology safely, respectfully and responsibly; recognise acceptable/unacceptable behaviour; identify a range of ways to report concerns about content and contact

W	Outcomes	Objectives
1	Can explain how to use technology safely. Can describe safety features that are included in internet browsers.	• To explain how to use a computer safely. • To know there are different types of browser. • To know that browsers have safety features included in them. • To describe why browsers have safety features.
2	Can discuss the advantages and disadvantages of internet filtering. Can show how to narrow an internet search by selecting different search criteria.	• To define internet filtering. • To know that schools may filter the content. • To discuss why filtering has advantages and disadvantages. • To know how to search using specific, appropriate keywords. • To explain how to narrow a search, by changing the search criteria.
3	Can be discerning in evaluating the content found using a search. Can use the search on a web page to locate particular words.	• To know how to search using specific, appropriate keywords. • To evaluate the results of a keyword search. • To be discerning in evaluating the content found using a search. • To know that particular words can be found on web pages, using a search tool. • To find particular words on a web page using the search tool.
4	Can compare the detailed and simple versions of *Wikipedia* to identify if the important information is present. Can model changing the bias and purpose of a website, using software tools.	• To know that there is *Wikipedia* and *Simple English Wikipedia*. • To explain the difference between *Wikipedia* and *Simple English Wikipedia*. • To discuss whether the important information is displayed in *Simple English Wikipedia* compared to *Wikipedia*. • To explain why there is a need for *Simple English Wikipedia*. • To know that wiki pages can be edited. • To be able to change the bias of a website by changing the text and images, using software tools.
5	Can present relevant information, in a concise way. Can evaluate other pupil presentations, using given criteria.	• To explain the importance of giving concise presentations, while including the important information. • To create criteria for an effective presentation. • To create a presentation based on effective, self-authored criteria. • To evaluate other children's presentations, based on self-authored criteria.
6	Can describe how websites may contain bias. Can choose and justify appropriate search keywords to locate information.	• To explain what bias is, through giving relevant examples. • To know that websites may contain bias. • To analyse websites to decide whether they are biased. • To explain how to choose appropriate search keywords and justify their selection.
Assess and review		• To assess the half-term's work.

Medium-term planning Spring 2: Michael Morpurgo

National Curriculum objective

Children should be taught to:
- select, use and combine a variety of software (including internet services) on a range of digital devices to design and create a range of programs, systems and content that accomplish given goals, including collecting, evaluating and presenting data and information

W	Outcomes	Objectives
1	Can describe how a piece of software has been designed for the user. Can design a simple questionnaire.	• To describe the difference between software and hardware. • To know that software is designed for particular users. • To describe how a piece of software is designed for particular users. • To explain how to complete a simple questionnaire. • To discuss what makes a good question. • To create a series of questions related to a particular author's work (for example, Michael Morpurgo).
2	Can use an online tool to create a simple questionnaire. Can explain the importance of human-computer interface design.	• To create a simple questionnaire, relating to an author (for example, Michael Morpurgo), using an online tool. • To review a simple questionnaire to decide if the questions can be answered using an online tool. • To describe the features of an online tool to identify the human-computer interface design. • To describe the importance of human-computer interface design.
3	Can use an online tool to collect questionnaire data. Can use an online tool to display questionnaire data.	• To use an online tool to collect questionnaire data. • To evaluate if the data is collected more efficiently using online tools compared to in-person. • To display the data gathered using an online tool, for different audiences.
4	Can use an online tool to create a questionnaire for two different audiences. Can collect and manipulate questionnaire data.	• To create a questionnaire, based upon a fictional book (for example, by Michael Morpurgo) using an online tool for two particular audiences. • To explain how a questionnaire can be designed for a particular audience. • To use an online questionnaire to collect data. • To manipulate data collected using an online tool.
5	Can examine and evaluate examples of infographics. Can create a simple infographic.	• To define an infographic. • To review examples of infographics and discuss their effectiveness, using given criteria. • To create a simple, paper-based infographic (themed upon a fictional book, for example, by Michael Morpurgo).
6	Can research a specific topic and present using an infographic. Can explain the importance of human-computer interface design.	• To create an infographic using online tools or software. • To research information, using a search engine, to locate information. • To present information in different ways as an infographic (themed upon a fictional book, for example, by Michael Morpurgo). • To explain the importance of human-computer interface design.
Assess and review		• To assess the half-term's work.

Medium-term planning Summer 1: Greek mythology

National Curriculum objectives

Children should be taught to:
- design, write and debug programs that accomplish specific goals, including controlling or simulating physical systems; solve problems by decomposing them into smaller parts
- use sequence, selection, and repetition in programs; work with variables and various forms of input and output
- use logical reasoning to explain how some simple algorithms work and to detect and correct errors in algorithms and programs

W	Outcomes	Objectives
1	Can understand what makes an effective maze game. Can plan a simple maze game using a given paper template.	• To identify what makes an effective maze game. • To establish their own criteria for effective maze games. • To brainstorm ideas for their own maze game based on a Greek Myth and develop one idea. • To identify an audience for their maze game. • To plan their maze game using a paper template. • To explain what elements they have included to ensure their maze game will be effective for the player.
2	Can plan and create the assets needed for their maze game. Can use multimedia tools to create appealing assets for their game.	• To identify the assets they need to create for their game. • To understand the importance of creating appealing assets within a game. • To consider what makes an appealing asset for their chosen audience. • To create sprites, backgrounds and sounds (their assets) for their animation as needed. • To carefully name their assets and understand why that is important.
3	Can use logical thinking to decompose their maze game into smaller parts. Can design and write programs to create a maze game.	• To decompose their game into smaller programmable parts. • To plan simply on paper the code for each part of their maze game. • To write their code for each part of their game. • To test and debug their code as they write it.
4	Can use simple post-test loops and two-way selection where appropriate. Can work collaboratively to test and debug their programs.	• To write their code for each part of their game. • To plan the use of sequences of two-way selection and post-test loops to create efficient programs. • To implement sequences of two-way selection and post-test loops to create efficient programs. • To work collaboratively to debug their code.
5	Can use multiple variables where appropriate to create an effective game. Can work collaboratively to test and debug their programs.	• To understand how multiple variables can be used to make their game more interesting for the player. • To use multiple variables to add scores, timers and lives as appropriate. • To test and debug their code as they write it. • To work collaboratively to debug their code.
6	Can evaluate their own and others' work. Can evaluate their own approach to the task.	• To give and receive constructive feedback. • To evaluate their own game and others' games using their own criteria, as determined in lesson one. • To discuss how they would change their approach if undertaking a similar task in the future.
Assess and review		• To assess the half-term's work.

Medium-term planning Summer 2: Shackleton and the South Pole

National Curriculum objectives

Children should be taught to:
- use search technologies effectively and be discerning in evaluating digital content
- use technology safely, respectfully and responsibly; recognise acceptable/unacceptable behaviour; identify a range of ways to report concerns about content and contact

W	Outcomes	Objectives
1	Can search effectively to locate information. Can evaluate digital content located via web searches.	• To know that search engines can be used to locate information. • To discuss the need for carefully choosing search keywords. • To share the results of a search and be discerning in the information that is located.
2	Can search for information using online maps.	• To search for particular given information, using an online mapping tool or software. • To use online mapping tool or software to locate a place visited by a great explorer, for example, Shackleton.
3	Can create personalised maps for a specific purpose. Can create a tour for a specific audience, using an online map.	• To know that online mapping tools can create a tour on a map. • To create a personalised map for a specific purpose. • To evaluate the scale and information shown on a personalised map. • To create a tour for a specific audience, using an online mapping tool.
4	Can retell a story using online maps. Can manipulate images of maps.	• To retell a story using an online map, for example, one of Shackleton's expeditions. • To manipulate images captured from an online mapping tool, to annotate important features.
5	Can plan an itinerary for a journey using online maps and related websites. Can evaluate digital content located via web searches.	• To plan an itinerary for a journey using online mapping tool. • To plan an itinerary for a journey using relevant websites. • To evaluate an itinerary for an expedition, using given criteria. • To create a presentation to describe an expedition, using online mapping tools and related websites. • To evaluate digital content located via web searches.
6	Can recognise acceptable behaviour online. Can identify ways to report concerns about content or contact.	• To describe acceptable behaviour online. • To know whom to contact, if someone behaves in an unacceptable manner online. • To know how to report concerns about content or contact online.
Assess and review		• To assess the half-term's work.

Year 5 Background knowledge

How computers work: an introduction to binary

Computers communicate with each other using binary code. People often associate long lists of ones and zeros with computer programming and will also be familiar with words like 'megabytes' or 'gigabytes' – all of which are linked to binary code. In binary code, numbers are represented only as a 0 or 1. In our decimal number system, we represent numbers as 0, 1, 2, 3, 4, 5, 6, 7, 8 and 9, i.e. ten different digits. It can be said therefore that binary is the number system, base 2, and the decimal system is base 10.

In decimal	0	1	2	3	4	5	6	7	8	9	10
In binary	0	1	10	11	100	101	110	111	1000	1001	1010

In base 10, we can place the digits into columns of hundreds, tens and ones, so then number 17 could be:

100s	10s	1s
0	1	7

$$(0 \times 100) + (1 \times 10) + (7 \times 1) = 17$$

In binary, base 2, the columns are labeled:

16s	8s	4s	2s	1s
1	0	0	0	1

$$(1 \times 16) + (0 \times 8) + (0 \times 4) + (0 \times 2) + (1 \times 1) = 17$$

So, using the binary number system the digits '10' represent $(1 \times 2) + (0 \times 1) = 2$ (see table above). Hence, the joke, *'There are only 10 people who understand binary, those who do and those who don't!'*

In order to get the children to understand binary, in the related 100s lessons, they play a 'Binary fingers' game. Two players face each other. They hold one hand behind their backs and hold up between 0 and 5 fingers. On the word 'Go' they show each other how many fingers they are holding up. The winner is the person to add up how many fingers there are in total and then say the binary number. For example, player 1 has 3 fingers, player 2 has 4 fingers, so the total is 7. This translates as $(0 \times 8) + (1 \times 4) + (1 \times 2) + (1 \times 1) = 111$ in binary.

Bits and bytes

The binary digits or 'bits' can be combined when sharing information. A 'byte' is a binary code containing 8 bits, e.g. 01101111. It is just a way of grouping the information. Using the 8 columns, means that combinations of numbers up to 11111111 can be stored (this is equivalent to the number 255 in decimal). The byte is a unit of digital information. Larger numbers of bytes can be called 'megabytes' (1,000,000 bytes) or 'gigabytes' (1000,000,000 bytes). Children like to hear of the terms for larger numbers and the system progresses from kilobyte, megabyte, gigabyte, terabyte, petabyte, exabyte, zettabyte to yottabyte. As technology improves so rapidly, these larger quantities of information may become more common in everyday language.

Packets of data

On the internet, every web page and email is sent and received as 'packets of data'. When an email is sent, the network breaks it into parts of a certain size (called a 'packet'). The packet contains the sender's address, the recipient's address, the total number of packets and the number of that individual packet. The packets are sent by the best route, so that they can get to their destination quickly and efficiently. Also, if there is a blockage on that route, the packets can go another way. All of the packets are brought together on the destination computer to form the web page or email.

■SCHOLASTIC

Year 6 Long-term planning

ALGORITHMS AND PROGRAMMING

The National Curriculum states that children should be taught to:

- design, write and debug programs that accomplish specific goals, including controlling or simulating physical systems; solve problems by decomposing them into smaller parts

- use sequence, selection, and repetition in programs; work with variables and various forms of input and output

- use logical reasoning to explain how some simple algorithms work and to detect and correct errors in algorithms and programs

---

- Children have been developing their algorithm and programming ability over the previous years. They need to continue to design, write and debug programs in multiple programming languages (visual or text-based).

- Children should be able to solve more complex problems by decomposing them into smaller parts.

- Even though children have used sequence, selection, and repetition in programs, they can now use more complicated arrangements of instructions.

- They work with variables using various forms of input and output.

- To increase efficiency, the children can explain and show how programs can use procedures or subroutines, within a program.

- Children should explain and show how programs can be planned, tested, corrected, and documented.

- In preparation for real-world applications, the children should be able to annotate programs with detailed comments.

- They should be able to look beyond a web browser to explain how HTML constructs the rendering of a web page.

- Developing their critical skills, they should review and assess the quality of code.

HOW COMPUTERS WORK

The National Curriculum states that children should be taught to:

- understand computer networks including the internet; how they can provide multiple services, such as the World Wide Web; and the opportunities they offer for communication and collaboration

- use technology safely, respectfully and responsibly

- The understanding of the key features of the World Wide Web and their relationships for example browsers, URLs and navigation methods, should continue to be developed.

DATA AND INFORMATION

The National Curriculum states that children should be taught to:

- select, use and combine a variety of software (including internet services) on a range of digital devices to design and create a range of programs, systems and content that accomplish given goals, including collecting, analysing, evaluating and presenting data and information

---

- Children can explain how computers represent all data in binary, for example, text representation, different sound and graphics file types.

- To understand real-world uses of data and information, the children need to be able to understand the need for the Data Protection Act and how it can affect them.

COMMUNICATION AND E-SAFETY

The National Curriculum states that children should be taught to:

- use search technologies effectively, appreciate how results are selected and ranked, and be discerning in evaluating digital content

- use technology safely, respectfully and responsibly; recognise acceptable/unacceptable behaviour; identify a range of ways to report concerns about content and contact

---

- Using the learning about networks, they should explain the role of search engines and what happens when a user requests a web page in a browser.

- Children should discuss social and ethical issues raised by the role of computers in the world.

- Developing prior learning, children should use search technologies effectively and be discerning in evaluating the located information.

- To prepare the children for working life beyond school, they should discuss career paths for those studying computing.

Overview of progression in Year 6

Algorithms and programming

During Year 6, the children consolidate their learning about algorithms and programming through longer, more complex projects. They design, write and debug programs for a specific project theme and are introduced to the Alice 2.4 program.

The children work with functions, two-way selection, loops and multiple-variables in their programming projects. The use of variables within programs links directly to the use of formulae and arithmetical rules in the mathematics curriculum.

The children have the opportunity to program using HTML in a web browser, to experience organising and manipulating the code to change the appearance of the web page. They also learn how the page is constructed, as the information is delivered via the internet.

Developing links with the English curriculum, the children can annotate their programs, with more detailed descriptions. They can also review and assess the quality of their code. In order to share this with their peers, the children can present their project, starting with their design brief, initial planning, development and user testing and critical feedback. The children can collaborate and work together in teams to complete the projects, so they need to understand roles and how to communicate clearly.

Data and information

The children revisit earlier learning about how sound files can be stored as .mp3 or .MIDI files and videos stored as .mov or .wmv files and connect the concept that larger files contain more data.

Through the projects, the children collect and present data using a variety of software to clearly deliver information for a specific audience.

The children are introduced to the Data Protection Act and discuss how it can affect them. They also consider copyright and Creative Commons, when sharing information online.

How computers work

The children have been learning about computer networks, the internet and the World Wide Web. They need to be able to describe the key features of these components and the relationships between them, for example, browsers, URLs and hyperlinks. They should experience different web browsers and identify the similarities and differences between them. The children will learn about what happens when a user requests a web page in a browser.

They should be able to describe the opportunities that the World Wide Web offers for communication and collaboration.

Communication and e-safety

Practically using search techniques, the children should demonstrate their knowledge and understanding of locating information. They should be clear explaining why they consider information to be reliable or potentially biased. They should have a simple understanding of how search results are ranked and also how they can be filtered to narrow a search.

In the final project, the children discuss the social and ethical issues raised by the role of computers in the world. This links with their learning in the English curriculum, where they use comparative language and create a discursive argument for a specific purpose.

Medium-term planning Autumn 1: Great Journeys

National Curriculum objectives

Children should be taught to:
- understand computer networks including the internet; how they can provide multiple services, such as the worldwide web; and the opportunities they offer for communication and collaboration
- use technology safely, respectfully and responsibly

W	Outcomes	Objectives
1	Can outline the key features of the World Wide Web. Can explain how to use a browser, including navigation via hyperlinks.	• To describe the internet in terms of a global network. • To describe the World Wide Web and how users connect. • To explain the difference between the World Wide Web and the internet. • To explain how to navigate web pages using a browser. • To explain a hyperlink and how it behaves. • To guide a peer through using a web page.
2	Can explain the relationship between different navigational methods. Can describe the features of large wikis, such as *Wikipedia* and how they are created and edited.	• To describe different navigational methods. • To explain the relationship between different navigational methods. • To name a large wiki, for example, *Wikipedia*. • To describe the features of a large wiki. • To explain how an entry on a large wiki is created and edited.
3	Can compare collaborating online and in-person. Can give examples of collaboration online using Web 2.0 tools.	• To identify the features of collaborating in person. • To identify the features of collaborating online. • To compare collaborating online and in person and give advantages and disadvantages. • To name examples of Web 2.0 tools. • To describe the workflow of using Web 2.0 tools for collaboration.
4	Can explain how a blog works. Can add a blog post and a comment.	• To identify the features of a physical diary. • To identify the features of a blog. • To know that a blog is a web log. • To be able to contribute a blog post. • To be able to evaluate a blog post contribution. • To comment upon a blog post in a positive manner.
5	Can use an online surveying tool and describe the advantages and disadvantages of using online tools.	• To identify online surveying tools. • To use an online survey tool to collect information. • To create a new survey to collect information. • To describe the advantages and disadvantages of online survey tools.
6	Can describe how computers can multitask. Can simply explain Moore's Law.	• To define 'multitasking' when associated with computers. • To know that computers can multitask. • To describe why multitasking is important. • To predict the future of computing, referring to Moore's Law. • To use technology safely and responsibly.
Assess and review		• To assess the half-term's work.

Medium-term planning Autumn 2: Fantasy worlds

National Curriculum objectives

Children should be taught to:
- design, write and debug programs that accomplish specific goals, including controlling or simulating physical systems; solve problems by decomposing them into smaller parts
- use sequence, selection, and repetition in programs; work with variables and various forms of input and output
- use logical reasoning to explain how some simple algorithms work and to detect and correct errors in algorithms and programs

W	Outcomes	Objectives
1	Can understand that problems can be solved in different ways. Can transfer knowledge and understanding about algorithms and programming to a second programming language.	• To solve problems using different methods. • To understand that there are many different programs that can be used to accomplish a task. • To use logical reasoning to determine how algorithms could be implemented with a different program and predict the outcome.
2	Can create algorithms to plan a number of different outcomes. Can execute algorithms using a second programming language.	• To understand the basic *Alice 2.4* interface. • To plan, create and test programs to solve a number of different challenges. • To know how to use templates to select a scene. • To know and understand how to add, orient and move objects in simple ways in *Alice 2.4*. • To explain to a beginner the *Alice 2.4* interface and how it can solve problems in different ways to *Scratch*.
3	Can plan a short story animation using a given template. Can add suitable assets to a program for their planned story animation.	• To design and plan a short animation using *Alice 2.4* based on *Alice in Wonderland*. • To give and receive constructive feedback. • To list the assets needed for their animation. • To use *Alice 2.4* to set the scene for their animation, selecting appropriate scenes and adding objects.
4	Can design and write a program to implement their short story plan. Can use loops (repetition) and selection to make their program more efficient.	• To plan the instructions needed by *Alice 2.4* to implement their short story plan. • To use *Alice 2.4* to create their planned program. • To test and debug their program as necessary. • To use loops and selection as needed within their program. • To explain how *Alice 2.4* differs from and is similar to *Scratch* in terms of how their algorithms are implemented.
5	Can add useful comments to their program. Can understand and explain that procedures can be used to make a program more efficient.	• To work collaboratively to test and debug their program. • To add suitable comments to their program. • To know and understand the term 'procedure'. • To explain how procedures are used in *Alice 2.4*.
6	Can present their work to their classmates. Can explain the importance of selecting the right program for a given purpose.	• To know how to save and export their animation and code so it can be viewed by anyone. • To present their animation to the class. • To give and receive constructive feedback. • To discuss the differences between *Scratch* and *Alice 2.4*. • To evaluate the use of both programs for different purposes.
Assess and review		• To assess the half-term's work.

Medium-term planning Spring 1: Africa

National Curriculum objectives

Children should be taught to:
- select, use and combine a variety of software (including internet services) on a range of digital devices to design and create a range of programs, systems and content that accomplish given goals, including collecting, analysing, evaluating and presenting data and information

W	Outcomes	Objectives
1	Can compare mobile phone apps and recognise common features. Can explain what the term 'User experience' means. Can decompose a larger problem into smaller parts.	• To know that the programs on mobile phones are known as apps and this is different to the phone's operating system. • To access apps and identify their purposes and common features. • To test apps and describe if the interface is easy to use for a Year 6 pupil. • To explain what the term 'user experience' means. • To describe the user experience for everyday activities. • To decompose a larger problem into smaller parts. • To discuss the needs of mobile phone users in Africa compared with the UK.
2	Can combine tools using app creation software to create a simple app. Can explain why user testing and feedback is important.	• To know that the programs on mobile phones are known as apps and this is different to the operating system. • To access apps and identify their purposes and common features. • To test apps and describe if the interface is easy to use for a Year 6 pupil. • To explain what the term 'User Experience' means. • To describe the user experience for everyday activities, in the UK. • To identify potential apps for users in Africa. • To decompose a larger problem into smaller parts.
3	Can improve an app design by responding to user feedback. Can annotate the app to explain the navigation and actions of the buttons.	• To know that the programs on mobile phones are known as apps and this is different to the operating system. • To access apps and identify their purposes and common features. • To test apps and describe if the interface is easy to use for a Year 6 pupil. • To identify a user in Africa and how the app is suitable for their needs. • To explain what the term 'User Experience' means. • To describe the user experience for everyday activities. • To decompose a larger problem into smaller parts.
4	Can explain why accessibility is important for an app. Can identify users who may need accessibility features.	• To know there are accessible features within apps. • To explain why accessibility is important for an app. • To identify users who may need accessibility features. • To explain how the accessibility features enable the person to use the app. • Discuss how the accessibility features could be similar or different for users in the UK and Africa.
5	Can identify how data may be collected within an app. Can simply explain the Data Protection Act.	• To know that apps can collect data. • To identify how apps can collect data. • To be able to give a simple explanation of the Data Protection Act.
6	Can give a simple definition of copyright. Can explain that there are different Creative Commons classifications. Can search for Creative Commons images.	• To be able to give a simple definition of copyright. • To know that image, text, video, games can be copyrighted. • To be able to give a simple definition of Creative Commons. • To explain that there are different Creative Commons classifications. • To be able to search for and locate appropriate Creative Commons images, for a specific purpose.
Assess and review		• To assess the half-term's work.

Medium-term planning Spring 2: Evacuees

National Curriculum objectives

Children should be taught to:
- use search technologies effectively, appreciate how results are selected and ranked, and be discerning in evaluating digital content
- use technology safely, respectfully and responsibly; recognise acceptable/unacceptable behaviour; identify a range of ways to report concerns about content and contact

W	Outcomes	Objectives
1	Can show how to perform a search using the 'Safe Search' filter. Can explain if they have concerns about content found during a search, who they should contact.	• To locate appropriate images using a search engine and 'Safe Search' filter. • To perform an advanced search to narrow the selection of images found. • To explain whom to contact if they have concerns about the content found during a search.
2	Can explain what happens when a user requests a web page in a browser. Can name different web browsers.	• To explain how web pages are delivered. • To name different web browsers. • To form analogies of sending and receiving information for web browsers, with war time codes.
3	Can evaluate how search results are ranked. Can decipher codes using an algorithm.	• To know that search results are delivered in different orders, based on rankings. • To describe that algorithms control the ranking of search results. • To use code breaking algorithms to decipher codes.
4	Can name common web address extensions for example, .com, .co.uk, .ac.uk and explain the types of organisations they represent. Can evaluate web pages for reliability.	• To be discerning in evaluating digital content, by looking at the web address extension. For example, .com, .ac.uk and identifying the organisations they represent. • To use analogies to consider misinformation during wartime, with misinformation from websites.
5	Can evaluate websites for bias using Web 2.0 tools. Can tag websites for bookmarking. Can identify advertising links on search websites and how cookies can be used.	• To evaluate websites for bias using given criteria. • To evaluate websites for bias using Web 2.0 tools. • To tag websites for bookmarking information. • To know that adverts appear on web pages. • To define a cookie. • To know that cookies are used on web pages to direct information to the user.
6	Can explain how to use a URL shortener and why they can reduce errors when entering addresses. Can recognise unacceptable behaviour and how to report it.	• To describe and name a URL shortener. • To know that URL shorteners can reduce errors when entering addresses. • To know how to report unacceptable behaviour and how to recognise it.
Assess and review		• To assess the half-term's work.

Medium-term planning Summer 1: Victorians

National Curriculum objectives

Children should be taught to:
- design, write and debug programs that accomplish specific goals, including controlling or simulating physical systems; solve problems by decomposing them into smaller parts
- use sequence, selection, and repetition in programs; work with variables and various forms of input and output
- use logical reasoning to explain how some simple algorithms work and to detect and correct errors in algorithms and programs

W	Outcomes	Objectives
1	Can evaluate video and online games to identify the 'good' gameplay features. Can describe the importance of a story to a game.	• To evaluate video and online games, using given criteria. • To discuss 'good' gameplay and modify evaluation criteria. • To describe the importance of a story to a game. • To identify common feature of game genres.
2	Can create a storyboard and flowchart for their game. Can plan and create the assets needed for their maze game.	• To use commercial video game examples to identify the main features of the plot. • To plan and create a storyboard for a new game. • To design a flowchart to describe the gameplay. • To identify the assets they need to create for their game. • To create sprites, backgrounds and sounds (their assets) for their animation as needed.
3	Can use logical thinking to decompose their maze game into smaller parts. Can design and write programs to create their game.	• To decompose their game into smaller programmable parts. • To plan simply on paper the code for each part of their game. • To write their code for each part of their game. • To test and debug their code as they write.
4	Can use simple post-test loops and two-way selection where appropriate. Can work collaboratively to test and debug their programs.	• To write their code for each part of their game. • To plan and implement the use of sequences of two-way selection and post-test loops to create efficient programs. • To work collaboratively to debug their code.
5	Can use multiple variables where appropriate to create an effective game. Can work collaboratively to test and debug their programs.	• To use multiple variables to add scores, timers, lives etc as appropriate. • To test and debug their code as they write it. • To work collaboratively to debug their code.
6	Can refine their game based on others' feedback. Can evaluate their own work and approach to the task.	• To give and receive constructive feedback. • To refine their game after receiving feedback from players and document the changes made. • To discuss how they would change their approach if undertaking a similar task in the future.
Assess and review		• To assess the half-term's work.

Medium-term planning Summer 2: Final project

National Curriculum objectives

Pupils should be taught to:
- design, write and debug programs that accomplish specific goals, including controlling or simulating physical systems; solve problems by decomposing them into smaller parts
- use sequence, selection, and repetition in programs; work with variables and various forms of input and output
- use logical reasoning to explain how some simple algorithms work and to detect and correct errors in algorithms and program.
- select, use and combine a variety of software (including internet services) on a range of digital devices to design and create a range of programs, systems and content that accomplish given goals, including collecting, analysing, evaluating and presenting data and information
- use search technologies effectively, appreciate how results are selected and ranked, and be discerning in evaluating digital content
- use technology safely, respectfully and responsibly; recognise acceptable/unacceptable behaviour; identify a range of ways to report concerns about content and contact

W	Outcomes	Objectives
1	Can modify a webpage using web tools. Can modify the webpage by changing the HTML. Can explain how a HTML webpage is structured.	• To modify a webpage using the Mozilla X-Ray goggles tool. • To observe the HTML language for text and images in a webpage. • To modify a webpage using the Mozilla Thimble tool, to alter the HTML. • To explain how a HTML webpage is structured.
2	Can use HTML to modify a webpage. Can combine software tools, to create a webpage using HTML. Can improve design by responding to user feedback.	• To modify a webpage using the Mozilla Thimble tool, to alter the HTML. • To create a webpage using the Mozilla Thimble tool. • To modify and improve a design, based on user feedback.
3	Can research and plan a project for a relevant, real-world problem. Can search the web, using appropriate search words. Can evaluate the information found.	• To identify a real-world problem which is relevant to the pupil. • To research a real-world problem using a search engine and appropriate search words. • To evaluate the information located using a search engine, using self-authored criteria.
4	Can plan a website, using flowcharts and wireframes. Can combine software tools, to create a website. Can explain why accessibility features are important.	• To plan and design a website, using flowcharts and wireframes. • To self-review a plan, before asking for feedback from others. • To combine software tools to create a website. • To decompose larger problems into smaller parts. • To know and explain why accessibility features are important.
5	Can discuss social and ethical issues raised by the role of computers in the world.	• To discuss the social and ethical issues raised by the role of computers in the world. • To consider social and ethical issues focused on the app, game or website produced.
6	Can discuss career paths in computing.	• To review the knowledge, skills and understanding of computing that they have developed over the key stage. • To discuss career paths in computing.
Assess and review		• To assess the half-term's work.

Year 6 Background knowledge

In Year 6, the curriculum builds and reinforces the knowledge over the years from Year 1. The children use new themes to practice their problem solving skills, using computational thinking.

Algorithms and programming

In Year 6, the children can use the text-based language HTML (Hypertext Markup Language). It consists of a series of tags that tell the browser how to display the web page. Hyperlinks can take the form of text or pictures that contain the links to other parts of a web page or another website.

HTML is written in plain text, so simple text programs, such as *Notepad*, can be used to edit it. More specific software for writing HTML can help to structure the writing or show how it is laid out (for example, *Sublime Text* http://www.sublimetext.com/).

There are rules to HTML; the HTML tags are surrounded by angled brackets < and >. Each page begins with <html> and ends with </html>. The second tag has a forward slash '/' to indicate that it is closing the <html> tag, it is similar to using brackets in English writing.

Every web page must contain the <html> and </html>, <head> and </head> and <body> and </body> tags. Think of it in a similar way to laying out a plan for a story or poster.

```
<html>
<head>

<title> This part is the HEAD of
the page </title>

</head>
```
```
<body>

This part is the BODY of the
page

All the text, pictures and other
parts are included here.

</body>
</html>
```

Further elements can be added, such as <h1> and </h1> for a large heading and <p> and </p> for a paragraph. It is good practice to comment on the code on a page, so that others can read and understand what that part of html is doing and also to help remind the author. Comments can be added as:

<!--This is a comment. Comments are not displayed in the browser when the page opens-->

In *100 Computing Lessons*, *Mozilla Thimble* is used as a tool to interest and excite the children about programming. The left-hand panel displays the code and the right-hand panel displays the web page. As the code is changed on the left, so the page changes on the right. There are many example projects available at the Webmaker website (http://webmaker.org). These ready-made projects encourage children to 'remix' the web and so learn through changing the example web pages.

Data and information

Data Protection Act

When considering personal information, adults and children must be careful how they share it and with whom. The Data Protection Act was designed to cover the storage of personal data on computer systems (made in 1984, revised in 1998). Personal data is data that relates to identifiable living individuals. Data must be acquired and processed lawfully and used for a specific purpose. For example, data collected for one purpose should not be used for marketing. The data should not be given to other organisations without consent. You will often find tick boxes on forms asking if you do not wish your details to be passed on.

Personal data should be accurate and up-to-date and people can request to see the data held about them, in order to check it. The data held should be the minimum required for the purpose. So, there is no justification for asking further questions for marketing purposes. Data should not be kept longer than is reasonable, so once its use has been completed, there is no reason to keep it forever. Data held on manual systems is not covered.

Finally, the data should be kept safely, so reasonable measures should be taken – for example, to prevent the data being accessed by hackers. Also, the data should be backed-up, in case of the technology breaking or being damaged by fire or flood.

Progression across the key stages

Algorithms and Programming

Year 1	Year 2
• To understand what algorithms are; how they are implemented as programs on digital devices; and that programs execute by following precise and unambiguous instructions.	• To understand what algorithms are; how they are implemented as programs on digital devices; and that programs execute by following precise and unambiguous instructions.
	• To create and debug simple programs.
	• To use logical reasoning to predict the behaviour of simple programs.
Explain that an algorithm is a way of solving a problem.	Explain that an algorithm is a precise way of solving a problem.
Know that algorithms can be followed by humans.	Know that algorithms can be followed by humans and computers.
Create algorithms with clear instructions.	Create algorithms with precise and clear instructions.
Give examples of algorithms in everyday life.	Give examples of algorithms in everyday life beyond school.
	Create and debug simple programs.
	Use logical reasoning to predict the behaviour of simple programs.

Year 3	Year 4	Year 5	Year 6
• To debug programs that accomplish specific goals, including controlling or simulating physical systems; solve problems by decomposing them into smaller parts.	• To write and debug programs that accomplish specific goals, including controlling or simulating physical systems; solve problems by decomposing them into smaller parts.	• To design, write and debug programs that accomplish specific goals, including controlling or simulating physical systems; solve problems by decomposing them into smaller parts.	• To design, write and debug programs that accomplish specific goals, including controlling or simulating physical systems; solve problems by decomposing them into smaller parts.
Debug programs created in a visual programming language.	Write and debug programs in a visual programming language.	Design, write and debug programs in multiple programming languages (visual or text-based).	Design, write and debug programs in multiple programming languages (visual or text-based).
Explain that computers are controlled by sequences of precise instructions known as programs.			Explain how HTML constructs the rendering of a web page.
Solve problems by decomposing them into smaller parts.	Solve problems by decomposing them into smaller parts.	Solve problems by decomposing them into smaller parts.	Solve problems by decomposing them into smaller parts.
• To use sequence and repetition in programs.	• To use sequence, selection, and repetition in programs; work with variables.	• To use sequence, selection, and repetition in programs; work with variables and various forms of input and output.	• To use sequence, selection, and repetition in programs; work with variables and various forms of input and output.
Explain and show how algorithms can use selection (if) and repetition (loops) in programs.	Explain and show how algorithms can use sequence, selection and repetition in programs.	Explain and show how algorithms can use sequence, selection and repetition in programs.	To effectively use sequence, selection, and repetition in programs.
	Work with variables within programs.	Work with variables and various forms of input and output.	Work with variables and various forms of input and output.

		Explain and show how programs can use procedures or subroutines, within a program.	Explain and show how programs can use procedures or subroutines, within a program.
• To use logical reasoning to explain how some simple algorithms work and to detect and correct errors in algorithms and programs.	• To use logical reasoning to explain how some simple algorithms work and to detect and correct errors in algorithms and programs.	• To use logical reasoning to explain how some simple algorithms work and to detect and correct errors in algorithms and programs.	• To use logical reasoning to explain how some simple algorithms work and to detect and correct errors in algorithms and programs.
Explain that computers need more precise instructions than humans and the need for precision to avoid errors.	Explain and use programs to simulate environments to test hypothesis.	Explain and show how programs can be planned, tested, corrected and documented.	Explain and show how programs can be planned, tested, corrected and documented.
Explain the need for accuracy of algorithms.	Distinguish between an algorithm and the programs that implement that algorithm.	To be able to annotate programs with simple comments.	To be able to annotate programs with detailed comments.
			Review and assess the quality of code.

Data and information

Year 1	Year 2
• To use technology purposefully to organise digital content.	• To use technology purposefully to create, organise, store, manipulate and retrieve digital content.
	Use technology purposefully to create digital content.
Use technology purposefully to organise digital content.	Use technology purposefully to organise digital content.
Use technology purposefully to manipulate digital content.	Use technology purposefully to manipulate digital content. Can manipulate data in graphical ways.
	Use technology purposefully to store digital content.
	Explain how the same information can be represented in a computer in a variety of ways for example, sound as mp3 or MIDI.

Year 3	Year 4	Year 5	Year 6
• To select, use and combine a variety of software to design and create a range of content that accomplish given goals, including collecting and presenting data and information.	• To select, use and combine a variety of software (including internet services) to create a range of content that accomplish given goals, including collecting and presenting data and information.	• To select, use and combine a variety of software (including internet services) on a range of digital devices to design and create a range of programs, systems and content that accomplish given goals, including collecting, evaluating and presenting data and information.	• To select, use and combine a variety of software (including internet services) on a range of digital devices to design and create a range of programs, systems and content that accomplish given goals, including collecting, evaluating and presenting data and information.
Explain that data can have errors, how this might affect results and decisions based on the data and how errors can be reduced.	Explain the importance of human-computer interface design.	Explain how the same binary data can be interpreted in different ways for example, an 8-bit value could be a character or a number.	Explain how computers represent all data in binary, with a variety of examples: unsigned integers, text representation (for example ASCII), different sound data/file types, and different graphics data/file types.
	Explain and use common troubleshooting techniques.	Explain the importance of human-computer interface design.	
		Explain how the same information can be represented in a computer in a variety of ways e.g. sound as mp3 or MIDI.	Explain the need for and content of the Data Protection Act, Computer Misuse Act and Copyright legislation (and other relevant legislation).

How computers work

Year 1	Year 2
• To recognise common uses of information technology beyond school.	• To recognise common uses of information technology beyond school.
Name devices that contain computers.	
Recognise common uses of computers in everyday life in school.	
Recognise common uses of computers in everyday life outside of school.	
Name the main parts of a computer and describe their function.	Explain and describe the key characteristics of basic computer architecture (for example, CPU, memory, hard disk, mouse, display etc).
	Explain how the same information can be represented in a computer in a variety of ways for example, sound as mp3 or MIDI.

Year 3	Year 4	Year 5	Year 6
• To understand computer networks and the opportunities they offer for communication and collaboration.	• To understand computer networks and the opportunities they offer for communication and collaboration.	• To understand computer networks including the internet; how they can provide multiple services, such as the World Wide Web; and the opportunities they offer for communication and collaboration.	• To understand computer networks including the internet; how they can provide multiple services, such as the World Wide Web; and the opportunities they offer for communication and collaboration.

Explain and describe the key characteristics of basic computer architecture (eg CPU, memory, hard disk, mouse, display etc).	Explain why there are sometimes different operating systems and application software for the same hardware.	Explain what the World Wide Web and the Internet are, and the difference.	Outline the key features of the World Wide Web and their relationships– eg browsers, URLs, navigation methods.
Explain why there are sometimes different operating systems and application software for the same hardware.	To communicate online using the internet and describe the opportunities for collaboration.	Outline how data are transported on the internet, including packets and the notion of a protocol.	Explain Moore's Law and multitasking by computers.

Communication and e-safety

Year 1	Year 2
• To keep personal information private; identify where to go for help and support when they have concerns about content or contact on the internet or other online technologies.	• To use technology safely and respectfully, keeping personal information private; identify where to go for help and support when they have concerns about content or contact on the internet or other online technologies.
Recognise what is personal information and keep it private.	Use technology safely and respectfully to communicate and to keep personal information private.
Know where to go for help and support when they have concerns about content on the internet.	Know where to go for help and support when they have concerns about content or contact on the internet.

Year 3	Year 4	Year 5	Year 6
• To use search technologies effectively.	• To use search technologies effectively and be discerning in evaluating digital content.	• To use search technologies effectively and be discerning in evaluating digital content.	• To use search technologies effectively, appreciate how results are selected and ranked, and be discerning in evaluating digital content.
Use search technologies to locate simple information.	Use search technologies to locate and evaluate information.	Use search technologies effectively and be discerning in evaluating the located information.	Use search technologies effectively and be discerning in evaluating the located information.
			Explain the role of search engines and what happens when a user requests a web page in a browser.
• To use technology safely, respectfully and responsibly; recognise acceptable/ unacceptable behaviour; identify a range of ways to report concerns about content and contact.	• To use technology safely, respectfully and responsibly; recognise acceptable/ unacceptable behaviour; identify a range of ways to report concerns about content and contact.	• To use technology safely, respectfully and responsibly; recognise acceptable/ unacceptable behaviour; identify a range of ways to report concerns about content and contact.	• To use technology safely, respectfully and responsibly; recognise acceptable/ unacceptable behaviour; identify a range of ways to report concerns about content and contact.
		Explain the technological perspective on safety and security.	Discuss career paths for those studying computing.
			Discuss social and ethical issues raised by the role of computers in the world.

Everything you need to
plan and teach the 2014 Curriculum

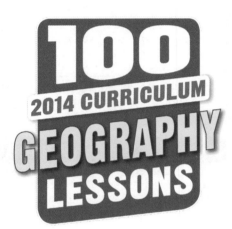

	RRP
Planning Guide	
978-1407-12861-0	£20.00
Year 1–2 *Available autumn 2014*	
978-14071-2856-6	£32.00
Year 3–4 *Available autumn 2014*	
978-1407-12857-3	£32.00
Year 5–6 *Available autumn 2014*	
978-1407-12858-0	£32.00

	RRP
Planning Guide	
978-1407-12860-3	£20.00
Year 1–2 *Available autumn 2014*	
978-1407-12853-5	£32.00
Year 3–4 *Available autumn 2014*	
978-1407-12854-2	£32.00
Year 5–6 *Available autumn 2014*	
978-1407-12855-9	£32.00

	RRP
Planning Guide	
978-1407-12859-7	£20.00
Year 1–2 *Available autumn 2014*	
978-1407-12850-4	£32.00
Year 3–4 *Available autumn 2014*	
978-1407-12851-1	£32.00
Year 5–6 *Available autumn 2014*	
978-1407-12852-8	£32.00

Find out more and order online at
www.scholastic.co.uk/100lessons